# SUEZ CRISIS 1956

## END OF EMPIRE AND THE RESHAPING OF THE MIDDLE EAST

DAVID CHARLWOOD

Pen & Sword
**MILITARY**

AN IMPRINT OF PEN & SWORD BOOKS LTD.
YORKSHIRE - PHILADELPHIA

First published in Great Britain in 2019 by
PEN AND SWORD MILITARY
*an imprint of*
Pen and Sword Books Ltd
47 Church Street
Barnsley
South Yorkshire S70 2AS

Copyright © David Charlwood, 2019

ISBN 978 1 52675 708 1

The right of David Charlwood to be identified as the author of this work
has been asserted in accordance with the Copyright, Designs and Patents Act 1988.

A CIP record for this book is available from the British Library All rights reserved.
No part of this book may be reproduced or transmitted in any form or by any means, electronic or
mechanical including photocopying, recording or by any information storage and retrieval system,
without permission from the Publisher in writing.

Every reasonable effort has been made to trace copyright holders of material reproduced in this book,
but if any have been inadvertently overlooked the publishers will be pleased to hear from them.

Front cover image: A Westland Whirlwind helicopter taking off from HMS *Albion*
Back cover image: Burning oil storage facilities in Port Said
Typeset by Aura Technology and Software Services, India
Maps and drawings by George Anderson
Printed and bound in England by TJ International Ltd., Padstow, Cornwall

Pen & Sword Books Ltd incorporates the imprints of Pen & Sword
Archaeology, Atlas, Aviation, Battleground, Discovery, Family History, History, Maritime, Military,
Naval, Politics, Railways, Select, Social History, Transport, True Crime, Claymore Press, Frontline
Books, Leo Cooper, Praetorian Press, Remember When, Seaforth Publishing and Wharncliffe.

*For a complete list of Pen and Sword titles please contact*
Pen and Sword Books Limited
47 Church Street, Barnsley, South Yorkshire, S70 2AS, England
email: enquiries@pen-and-sword.co.uk
website: www.pen-and-sword.co.uk

or
Pen and Sword Books
1950 Lawrence Rd, Havertown, PA 19083, USA
email: uspen-and-sword@casematepublishers.com
www.penandswordbooks.com

# CONTENTS

| | |
|---|---|
| Maps | 4 |
| Timeline | 6 |
| Prologue | 8 |
| 1. Seizure | 12 |
| 2. Colonialists and Fascists | 18 |
| 3. The View from the East | 25 |
| 4. Satisfaction | 33 |
| 5. A Swim from Malta | 39 |
| 6. An Invitation | 43 |
| 7. To the United Nations | 49 |
| 8. *Casus Belli* | 54 |
| 9. Sèvres | 58 |
| 10. "A Nail in My Head" | 62 |
| 11. The Jordanian Complication | 67 |
| 12. Storms in the Desert | 72 |
| 13. From Russia, with Love | 82 |
| 14. Resolution 997 | 89 |
| 15. Election Day | 97 |
| 16. Black Gold and Blue Helmets | 106 |
| Epilogue: The Curse of the Pharaohs | 110 |
| Afterword: The Parallels of Suez and Iraq | 115 |
| Sources | 120 |
| Index | 126 |

## Suez Crisis 1956

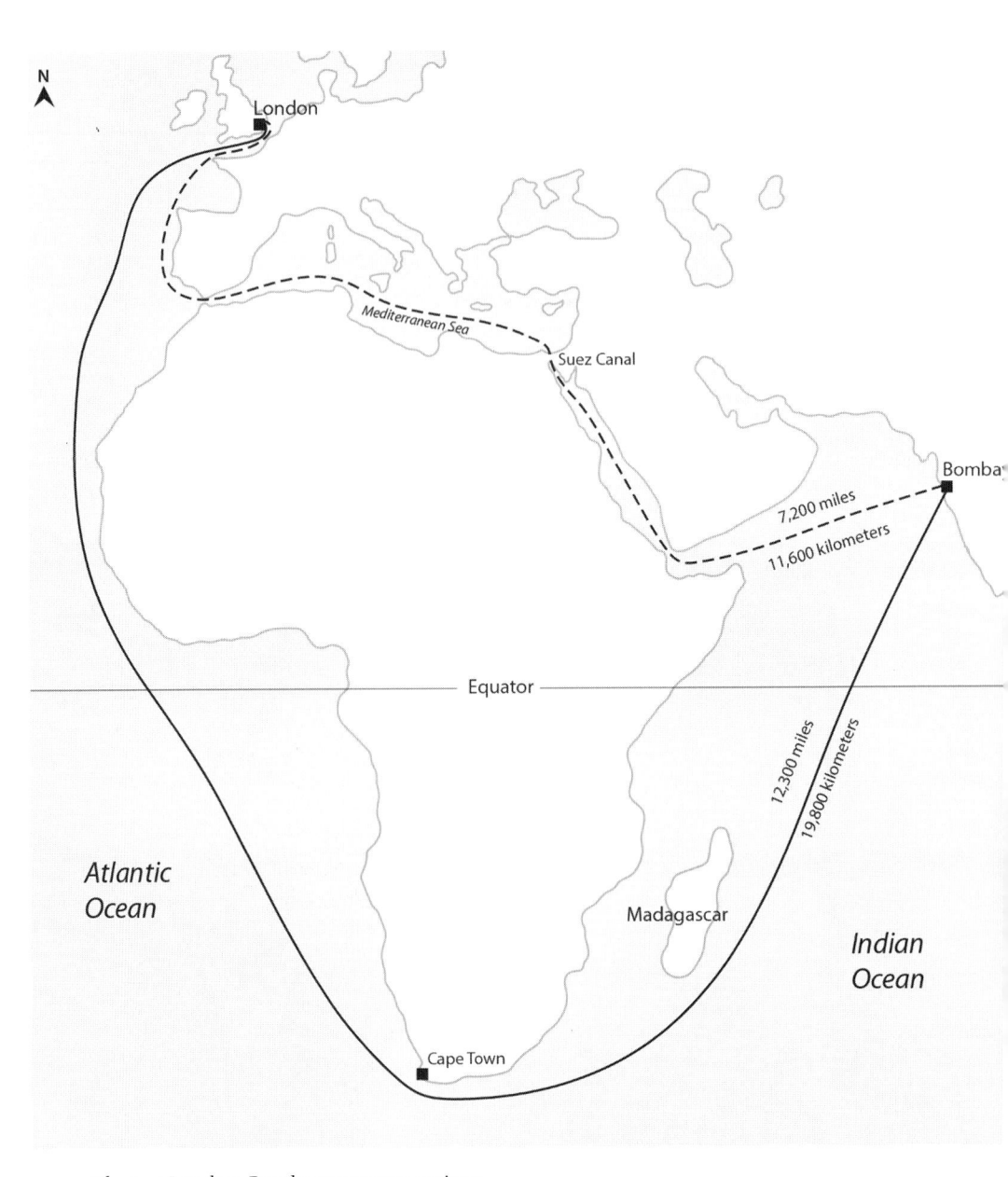

The two London–Bombay sea route options.

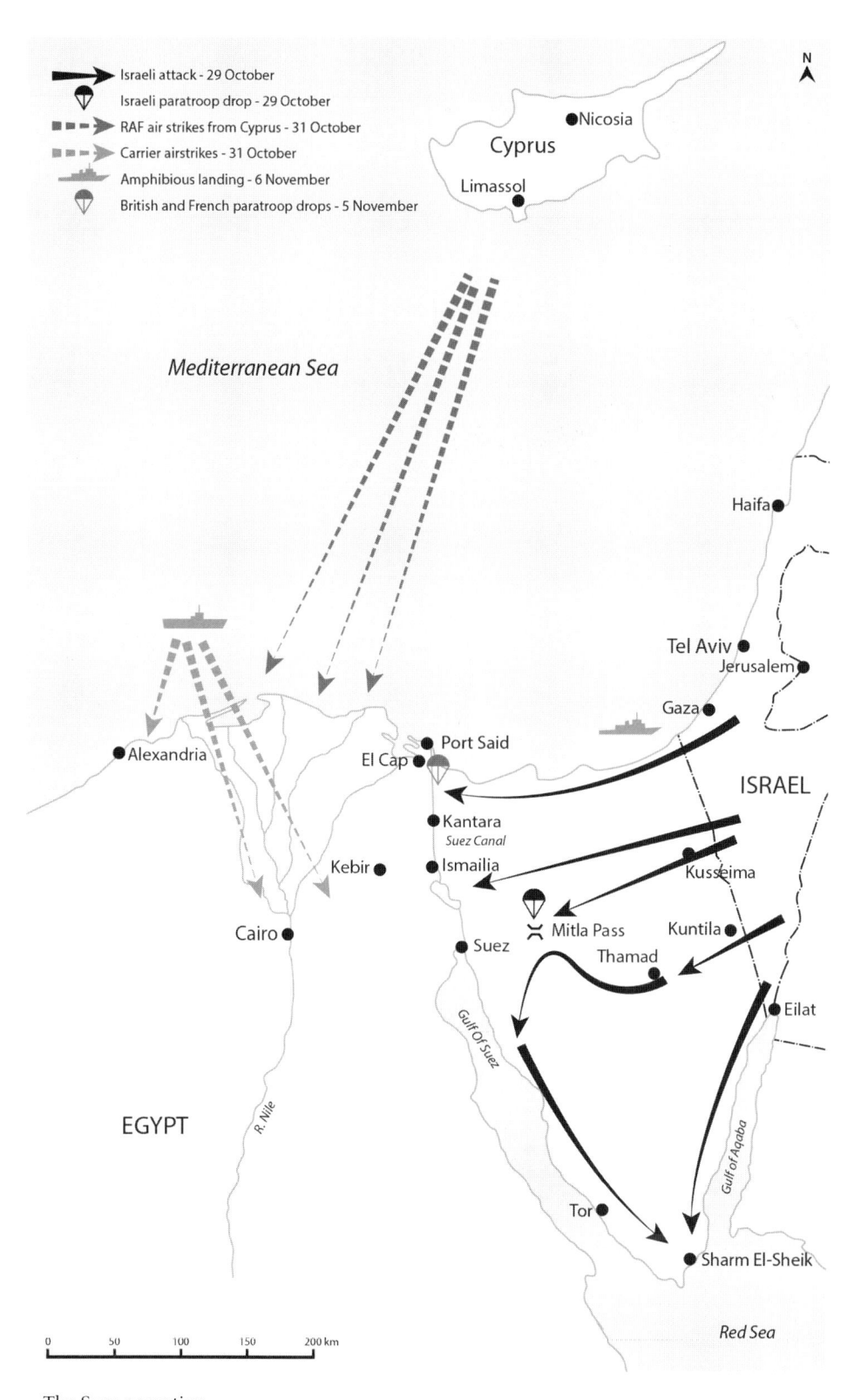

The Suez operation.

# TIMELINE

**1955**

September — Nasser agrees arms deal with Czechoslovakia for Soviet-made weaponry

21 November — U.S., Britain and Egypt begin discussions over financing for the Aswan Dam

**1956**

13 June — Last British forces depart from Suez Canal Base in line with the 1954 Anglo-Egyptian Treaty

19 July — U.S. Secretary of State Dulles informs the Egyptian ambassador that U.S. will not fund construction of the Aswan Dam

26 July — Nasser nationalizes the Suez Canal

12 August — Nasser rejects invitation to attend the London conference

18 August — Start of the Conference of London

5 September — Nasser rejects Menzies' proposals of internationalization of the Suez Canal

15 September — European pilots leave the Suez Canal. Egypt maintains traffic using Egyptian, Russian and Indian pilots

19 September — Start of second London conference to discuss American proposal for Suez Canal Users' Association (SCUA)

5–13 October — UN Security Council debates Suez Crisis

14 October — Eden meets French representatives at Chequers who present the plan to use Israeli invasion as pretext for attack

24 October — Britain, France and Israel sign Sèvres Protocol

29 October — Israeli forces attack Egypt

30 October — British and French issue ultimatum to Egypt and Israel

31 October — Royal Air Force begins bombing of Egyptian targets

5 November — French and British airborne troops land at Port Said

6 November — British and French amphibious forces land at Port Said and that evening Eden agrees ceasefire; Eisenhower wins re-election

*Timeline*

| 7 November | Eisenhower messages Ben-Gurion demanding withdrawal of Israeli forces |
| 3 December | Lloyd announces intention to withdraw all British forces from Suez. |
| 20 December | Eden states in Parliament that he had no foreknowledge of the Israeli attack on Egypt |
| 23 December | Last British and French troops leave Suez |

**1957**

| 5 January | Eisenhower presents the 'Eisenhower Doctrine' to U.S. Congress |
| 9 January | Eden resigns as prime minister |
| 13 March | Jordan pulls out of Anglo-Jordanian Treaty |
| 8 April | Suez Canal reopens |
| 13 July | Suez Canal Company reaches compensation agreement with Egyptian government |

The entrance to the canal at Port Said, 1869.

# PROLOGUE

On Christmas Eve 1798, Napoleon Bonaparte stared out across the sea of sand between Cairo and Suez. France's most famous general carried with him an order to begin an engineering project to open up new trade routes in the East. He was simply instructed to "arrange for the cutting of the Isthmus of Suez".

The idea of carving a path through the strip of land that separated the Mediterranean and the Red Sea had been dreamed of as far back as the Pharaohs, but would consume the sleepless nights of emperors and engineers for another seventy years before it was finally completed at a cost of hundreds of thousands of lives and millions of dollars. The plaudits for the creation of the canal went to another Frenchman: Ferdinand de Lesseps.

De Lesseps was a bushy-moustached and indefatigable career diplomat who only began trying to build a canal after he had officially retired. He had no engineering qualifications. He did, however, have a diplomat's ability to win friends and influence people, including Said Pasha, who ruled Egypt as viceroy, nominally under the auspices of the Ottoman sultan. De Lesseps returned to his old diplomatic haunt in 1854 and convinced Said Pasha to back the scheme by appealing to his sense of ego: "What a fine claim to glory! For Egypt, what an imperishable source of riches!" Somewhat inaccurately he added, "The names of those Egyptian sovereigns who built the pyramids ... are forgotten. The name of the Prince who opens the great maritime canal will be blessed from century to century until the end of time." Said Pasha agreed and granted a 'concession' to the newly created Compagnie universelle du canal maritime de Suez to control the planned waterway for ninety-nine years following construction, after which time ownership would revert to the Egyptian government. With the concession agreed, de Lesseps went off to find financial backers.

The concept was a potentially lucrative one. By cutting a canal between the Mediterranean and the Red Sea, vessels travelling between Europe and Asia would

Ferdinand de Lesseps.

no longer have to sail around the Cape of Good Hope at the southern tip of Africa and whoever was part of the concession would get a cut of the fee every vessel transiting the canal would be required to pay. The problem was not one of potential profit, however, but one of practicalities. Even though de Lesseps had the backing of a team of experienced engineers, it would still be a herculean task. Selling the project was not helped by the fact that Napoleon's own engineers, when they had investigated the potential of a canal in the late eighteenth century, had wrongly calculated that the Red Sea was ten metres higher than the Mediterranean and that cutting a path between the two would result in catastrophic flooding across the Nile Delta and the manmade river becoming a raging, unnavigable torrent. Even though de Lesseps's engineers were right and Napoleon's wrong, it was hard to cast aside the notion that the scheme was liable to failure, but the British objections were primarily over security. Britannia ruled the waves in the nineteenth century and even though relations with France were cordial, the British in particular did not trust the French; as one minister told de Lesseps, in the event of war with France both ends of the canal would be closed to Britain and it would be "a suicidal act on the part of England" to support the venture.

In Paris, de Lesseps came up against personal and technical objections, but, undaunted, began a campaign to change peoples' minds. He established an international commission to affirm the soundness of the engineers' plans, mounted a publicity campaign that got the backing of maritime businesses and set up a shareholding side of the company. Lord Palmerston, Britain's prime minister, fought tooth and nail, damning the canal as "among the many bubble schemes that from time to time have been palmed upon gullible capitalists", but in

The statue of de Lesseps on the Port Said waterfront would be one of the designated landing points for British helicopter-borne troops.

November 1858, shares of the Suez Canal Company went on sale. More than half were taken up in France, significantly by the general public and small investors, and de Lesseps turned to his friend Said Pasha, whom he persuaded to part with the eyewatering sum of £3.5 million to cover the 44 per cent remaining unsold. De Lesseps had his money.

Construction of the canal began in April 1859. Opinion in London was still sceptical and *The Times* found itself insulting "the French or any other people ... bent upon sinking their money in the sand" while simultaneously claiming:

> If, however, contrary to all probabilities, the project should actually be realized, we can only say that the canal will be so far a British Canal ... traversed by British ships, devoted to British traffic and maintained by British tolls.

The project proved profoundly labour intensive. Along with his concession on ownership, de Lesseps had persuaded the naïve viceroy to agree to supply Egyptian labour to help construct the canal. Digging with minimal tools, as many as 120,000 Egyptians, many of whom were forced labourers, died to cut a path between the seas. In the end, the canal took ten years to construct and ran massively over budget, but when it was finally completed, the 64-year-old de Lesseps had become an international celebrity.

At the opening of the canal in 1869 he received a congratulatory message from the British Foreign Office which commended his "indomitable perseverance" in the face of "physical circumstances and of a local state of society to which such undertakings

An artist's impression of the night illuminations on the day of the opening of the Suez Canal.

were unknown". The waterway was, in the words of one British admiral, "a work of vast magnitude, conceived and carried out by the energy and perseverance of M. Lesseps."

Six years later, a new British prime minister – Benjamin Disraeli – persuaded the now near-bankrupt Egyptian government to sell its share of the canal concession and ownership entirely passed out of Egyptian hands. It was a moment that sowed seeds of resentment which would bear a bitter fruit. The country maintained its nominal position as part of the Ottoman Empire, but was now massively indebted. European officials – acting on behalf of Egypt's creditors – had taken control of the country's finance and public works and resentment spilled into a nationalist uprising backed by the army in 1882. Britain sent an army to restore order, order which in part needed to be maintained to safeguard access to the canal, the traffic of which was 70 per cent British. One of the gloomy predictions of Palmerston, already long consigned to the grave, had come to pass: "If it [the canal] is made there would be a war."

Even though Egypt became officially independent in 1922, British troops stayed to guard the crucial canal, which was still joint-owned by British and French shareholders and had been declared a neutral, international waterway. The importance of access to India decreased over time, with India granted independence from British rule in 1947, but the canal instead became Britain's lifeline for oil from the Gulf; the year before the crisis, 76 per cent of the traffic from the Red Sea to the Mediterranean was oil and 20 per cent of it was destined for Britain. The sanctity of shipping was now the primary concern; as Winston Churchill grandly and not entirely truthfully told American journalists during a trip to the U.S. in 1952, "Now that we no longer hold India the Canal means very little to us … We are holding the Canal not for ourselves, but for Civilization."

The reality on the ground was more complex. 'Holding' the canal entailed the presence of thousands of British soldiers and between 1950 and 1956, fifty-four servicemen were killed in violent attacks. De Lesseps's promise that the canal would become a "fine claim to glory" and an "imperishable source of riches" for Egypt had proved rather hollow. By the 1950s, far from being a symbol of human endeavour, the waterway had become a symbol of Western imperialism.

# 1. SEIZURE

On a sweltering summer evening in Alexandria on 26 July 1956, Egypt's new president stepped up to a bank of waiting microphones to give the most famous speech of his life. A crowd had crammed into Menishiya Square, sweatily jostling for position as the former army colonel-turned-president raised both arms in greeting to his listeners. Gamal Abdel Nasser wore a suit rather than his military uniform, but he still carried himself like a soldier: broad shoulders back, hair close-cropped above an officer's moustache. He spoke passionately, frequently raising his clenched left fist at the lectern to emphasize his words. He related the history of the canal, of Egypt's occupation by the British since 1882, of other wrongs. Voice raised, he urged the crowd,

> Britain has forcibly grabbed our rights ... The income of the Suez Canal Company in 1955 reached 35 million pounds, or 100 million dollars. Of this sum, we, who have lost 120,000 persons, who have died in digging the Canal, take only one million pounds or three million dollars ... We shall not repeat the past. We shall eradicate it by restoring our rights in the Suez Canal.

In short, Nasser asserted Suez was "an Egyptian Canal" and he intended to take it back. While he spoke, Egyptian forces seized control of the canal and the Canal Company's offices. The coded phrase for the operation to begin was Nasser's mention of the name of the waterway's architect: de Lesseps.

That evening, British Prime Minister Anthony Eden was hosting a formal dinner at Downing Street. After an aide brought in the news from Egypt the meal ended early and Eden held an emergency meeting with a few of his Cabinet ministers which went on until 4 a.m. Nasser's action was, as *The Times* phrased it the following morning, "a clear affront and threat to Western interests, besides being a breach of undertakings which Egypt has freely given". The Egyptian president's takeover of the canal was a potential threat to Britain's oil supplies, as the country only had six weeks' reserves, and it was also a profound embarrassment to the nation which had been joint custodian of the canal since its creation and whose soldiers had, until a few weeks before, been its guardians. A determined Eden sent a courteous but clear message across the Atlantic to the White House: "my colleagues and I are convinced that we must be ready, in the last resort, to use force to bring Nasser to his senses. For our part we are prepared to do so."

The Suez Crisis had begun.

Nasser's seizure of the Suez Canal was not just a shock to politicians in Britain. When Nasser informed his own ministers on the morning of 26 July what he planned to say in his speech that evening, most sat in stunned silence before asking nervous questions.

Nasser addresses the crowd in Menishiya square. He was an articulate and impassioned speaker.

The Suez Canal at Ismalia.

One told Nasser that if he went ahead, "This decision means that we shall become directly involved in a war with Britain, France and the whole of the West."

Nasser was unperturbed and replied, "I did not ask you to fight. If war breaks out it will be Abdul Hakim Amir [the Egyptian Army chief of staff] who will be fighting, not you."

Even for his own ministers, Nasser's plan to take the canal by force seemed an extreme reaction, but the crisis had been brewing for decades.

The flamboyant nineteenth-century poet and playwright Oscar Wilde quite neatly summed up the canal conundrum. In his 1895 comedy *The Ideal Husband* – which rather appropriately examines corruption in high politics – one character who is a minister at the Foreign Office remarks, the Suez Canal was a very great and splendid undertaking. It gave us our direct route to India. It had imperial value. It was necessary that we should have control. The comment was a moment of comparative light comedy, but it was a devoutly held view among most of the British establishment for the better part of a century. Anything but British control of the waterway was almost unimaginable. As Eden summarized it in 1929, twenty-six years before he became prime minister,

> If the Suez Canal is our back door to the East, it is the front door to Europe and Australia, New Zealand and India. If you like to mix your metaphors it is, in fact, the swing-door of the British Empire, which has got to keep continually revolving.

Nasser was now threatening to jam the door shut.

The problematic issue with keeping the Suez door revolving was that under the terms of agreements already made with the Egyptians, British troops were required to leave by 1956 anyway. And the cost of keeping them there was astronomical. Maintaining control of the canal was expensive and flagrantly imperialist, but the alternative was to risk potential disruption to shipping and the security of Britain's oil supplies. However, one of the facts often ignored by many historians and commentators is that perhaps the greatest exponent of a more realistic Suez Canal policy on the part of the British government prior to 1956 was Anthony Eden.

Eden would go on to be widely regarded as Britain's worst prime minister in modern history, almost entirely because of the Suez Crisis, but the charming, erudite, upper-class Etonian and Oxford graduate was in fact viewed by most as a popular, consummate diplomat when he finally became prime minister in 1955.

Eden had been foreign secretary under Winston Churchill throughout Churchill's terms in office as prime minister, both during the Second World War and in the 1950s. He began as a firm proponent of the establishment view of the canal and of protecting Britain's interests military, but over time adopted a more pragmatic desire to reduce

British Prime Minister Anthony Eden with his wife Clarissa.

Britain's role. In 1952, while foreign secretary, he wrote a classified memorandum for Cabinet which stated,

> it is clearly beyond the resources of the United Kingdom to assume the responsibility alone for the security of the Middle East. Our aim should be to make the whole of this area and in particular the [Suez] Canal Zone an area of international responsibility.

Far from being an idle whim, the policy of making responsibility for Suez international was one which Eden at least publicly held to for the duration of the crisis and the remainder of his life. The main opposition to his desire to reduce Britain's commitment in fact came from Winston Churchill. During a fiery Cabinet meeting in the midst of negotiations with Egypt in 1954, Eden pointedly told Churchill in front of his Cabinet colleagues, "In the second half of the twentieth century we cannot hope to maintain our position in the Middle East by the methods of the last century. However little we like it, we must face that fact."

Eden, supported by Cabinet, prevailed and in 1954 he persuaded Egypt's new leader, Gamal Abdel Nasser, to sign the Anglo-Egyptian Treaty, which agreed to the withdrawal of British military forces by 1956, but maintained the canal as an international waterway and the Canal Company in British and French hands. It seemed a perfectly reasonable solution; indeed Nasser himself had told the British newspaper the *Daily Mirror* a few months before the agreement was concluded, "If this question [of the presence of British forces] were settled, a great friendship could exist between us [Britain and Egypt]."

In March 1956 the last British unit, the 2nd Battalion of The Grenadier Guards, departed from Port Said with the final troops leaving in June. The much-angsted-over decision to withdraw British forces was an entirely pragmatic one, but one which even caused its architect concern. In a communication with U.S. President Dwight D. Eisenhower, Eden described the military withdrawal as "an act of faith in Egypt". It was not a widely held faith: as one Conservative MP remarked, "the recent conduct of Colonel Nasser gives nobody any grounds for confidence in him as custodian of an international waterway."

Nasser also had his own concerns that went beyond the unappealing sight of khaki-clad foreigners standing guard over Egypt's canal. He had come to power in Egypt through a military coup in 1952 and found himself in charge of a nation with huge domestic problems. The new world into which he led Egypt was one divided between

Buildings in the Suez Canal zone, 1910.

East and West, capitalism and Communism and Egypt was at the centre of the contested region of the Middle East and the location of the crucial canal. Across the world, nations were aligning themselves in the Cold War and when Nasser came to power, conflicts in which combatants were ideologically divided and supported by either Moscow or Washington were raging in Korea and Indochina (Vietnam). Astutely, Nasser played both sides. He purchased Soviet-made weapons via an arms deal with Czechoslovakia while courting the World Bank and the U.S. and Britain for funding for his grand plans to build a dam across the Nile River at Aswan. The project was expected to cost more than a billion dollars. The funding came with the condition that Nasser refuse any aid from the Communist Bloc, but the U.S. State Department decided to use the U.S. chequebook as a weapon to coerce Nasser to align with the West. Apparently out of the blue, although there was mounting domestic political pressure against the Americans paying for an Egyptian dam, the U.S. unilaterally pulled the plug on their part of the funding, collapsing the whole deal. The Egyptian ambassador in Washington was hauled in to see the secretary of state and summarily told the deal was off. As Eden politely later recorded in his memoirs, "We were informed but not consulted and so had no prior opportunity for criticism or comment" – the British prime minister found out from an aide who was reading the Reuters ticker tape – adding, "the news was a wounding to his [Nasser's] pride."

The cancellation of the funding for the Aswan Dam was the immediate trigger for Nasser's decision to take control of the Suez Canal a week later. It perplexed the French foreign minister in particular, as it was the Americans who had killed off the stillborn dam project: "we could not see any reason why Egypt should attack Franco-British interests to avenge itself against an affront inflicted by the United States."

Nasser cared little for such nuance. To the jubilant crowds crushed close together in the square in Alexandria on the evening of 26 July, he announced that the fees taken from ships transiting the canal would be used to build the dam: "We will build the [Aswan] High Dam and we will get all the rights we lost ... [and] destroy once and for all the traces of occupation and exploitation."

# 2. COLONIALISTS AND FASCISTS

In Washington, the perspective on the entire situation was rather different to that in London. Eden's emergency message to Eisenhower had told the president that Nasser's action constituted an "immediate threat" to Western Europe's oil supplies, but for all the bombastic nationalism of Nasser's move on the canal, the response was not clear cut. The Suez Canal Company was and always had been registered as an Egyptian company and Nasser had promised to compensate the shareholders at market prices for the takeover by the state; the fact was even admitted in the first full meeting of the British Cabinet after Nasser's announcement, where it was noted in the minutes, "from the strictly legal point of view, his [Nasser's] action amounts to no more than a decision to buy out shareholders."

Even the takeover itself was a rather underwhelming moment: an Egyptian captain who was part of the group that entered the Canal Company offices on the night of 26 July later recalled, "we found the French and British and Greeks [employees]

The Suez Canal Company's offices were located on the waterfront at Port Said.

were very friendly. We told them, 'The Canal is nationalized. It belongs to Egypt now. We want your cooperation. The ships must go on moving in the Canal.' Then we exchanged cigarettes."

Nasser's action was a shock, but it was not illegal under international law and if the original terms of the de Lesseps canal arrangement were upheld the concession would revert to Egyptian ownership by 1969 in any event. There was outrage in London and Paris, but in Washington, Eisenhower was rather more sanguine. When he first received warning from the chargé d'affaires in London that military action was being considered by Eden's government he responded that nationalizing the canal "was not the same as nationalizing oil wells" which would run out; rather, the canal was more like a "public utility". From the outset there was a strong sense in Washington that the response in Britain and France was out of proportion.

U.S. president and former wartime general Dwight D. Eisenhower.

It also played into a broader post-war narrative that the old empires were an anachronism that hindered U.S. policy. When U.S. Secretary of State John Foster Dulles visited Egypt in 1955 he noted acidly,

> Such British troops as are left in the area are more a factor of instability rather than stability ... The association of the U.S. in the minds of the people of the area with French and British colonial and imperialistic policies are millstones around our neck.

The president was determined that U.S. foreign policy, and more particularly his own ambitions to secure a second term in elections scheduled that autumn, would not drown in the shallow waters of the Suez Canal, dragged under by the millstone of British and French hubris.

On 31 July, Eisenhower held a private meeting with Dulles and a few key military men in which he asserted the British idea of a military response was "out of date ... as a mode of action". The U.S. view of Nasser's Egypt was a complex one. Eisenhower to some extent claimed to understand Nasser's motivation, admitting, "Nasser embodies the emotional demands of the people of that area for independence." But he was clear that Nasser should be "made to disgorge his theft", citing that the U.S. did not want to see the Panama Canal nationalized.

In the context of the Cold War, there was grave concern in Washington that Egypt would end up in the Soviet camp, an eventuality made seemingly more likely by Nasser's September 1955 arms deal with Czechoslovakia in which Egypt secured a package of 100 Russian-made MiG fighter jets, 200 tanks and a number of bombers in exchange for shipments of Egyptian cotton.

Eisenhower heard about the Czech arms deal while he was on holiday playing golf in Colorado. He was dragged off the course to answer a call from Dulles

The uncompromising U.S. Secretary of State John Foster Dulles, a former Wall Street lawyer, who died three years after the Suez Crisis.

Russian-made arms purchases from Czechoslovakia on display in Egypt in 1956.

who told his president that the Egyptians were going to obtain "a massive lot of arms" from the Soviets. The U.S. National Security Council (NSC) simultaneously reported that the Soviets were "accelerating their activities in the Middle East", but the perception in Washington was that Nasser could be cajoled and bribed into staying out of the Cold War. The month after Nasser agreed his Soviet arms deal, Secretary of State Dulles asserted, "We do not want to lose Arab goodwill unless Arabs themselves in conspiracy with the Soviets force this upon us."

Nasser espoused an ideology of Pan-Arabism – a nationalist notion connecting all Arabs across the Middle East through their shared culture – and what happened in Egypt had the potential to destabilize the entire region. The same year that Nasser bought his MiGs, Iraq, Iran, Turkey and Pakistan were persuaded to agree the 'Baghdad Pact' with Great Britain. Under the guise of upholding the United Nations' charter all five nations committed to "the maintenance of peace and security", an act which in reality aligned them on the side of the West in the Cold War.

It was no coincidence that the member nations were arranged like a buffer between the southern borders of the USSR and the location of British oil interests. Turkey's foreign minister asserted that Nasser's arms deal "had created a new and dangerous situation in the Middle East", adding, "the most effective way of dealing with it was to isolate Egypt by regrouping remaining Arab states firmly around the Baghdad Pact."

While the Baghdad Pact in principle supported Western interests, Eisenhower saw it as a blunt instrument. The U.S. refused to join the pact and dissuaded the British from trying to increase membership, while becoming increasingly frustrated that British action in the region was assumed to be undertaken at the blessing and behest of Washington. In January 1956, Eisenhower confided in his diary, "The Arabs apparently take the assumption that Britain does nothing in this area [the Middle East] without our approval. Nothing could be further from the truth."

The Aswan Dam provided an opportunity to bring Nasser to heel. The broad plan, as defined by the U.S. State Department, was to "induce reorientation of Nasser's policies toward cooperation with the Free World while lessening the harmful Egyptian influence in other countries of the Middle East". U.S. and British policies were now diverging, with the Foreign Office suggesting the U.S. effort was a complete waste of time; the State Department minuted, "The UK is strongly of the opinion that the West can reach no accommodation with Nasser." The U.S. was already providing extensive aid to Egypt and this was gradually cancelled, while it was decided that funding for the dam would also be ended, in part because of rising domestic political opposition.

On 19 July 1956, Dulles met the Egyptian ambassador in Washington and lamented what he described as a lack of "goodwill" from Cairo. The ambassador pointed out that Egypt could always look to the Soviets for economic support and in response Dulles stunned the ambassador by announcing the entire deal was off. The State Department theory, which was supported by Eisenhower, was that Nasser would eventually see sense and cease his Eastward charm offensive.

Eisenhower's calm response to Nasser's nationalizing of the Suez Canal arguably stemmed from the fact that the Washington view was that the Egyptian leader was simply throwing his toys out of the pram, whereas in London, the action was seen as a clear and present danger to Western interests.

To hold off the suggestion of immediate British military action in July, Dulles was dispatched to London to propose that an international conference should take place to resolve the situation. The president and his advisers were still of the view that Nasser should not be allowed to get away with it and the planned response was to implement "policies designed to reduce Nasser as a force in the Middle East". However, the idea of going to war of over Nasser's tantrum was a complete anathema.

A British diplomat in Washington conveyed the clear message from Dulles: "he agreed that our attitude should be a firm one … [but] his view was that so long as there was no interference with the navigation of the canal … there was no basis for military action." Musing on the outcome of a conflict, Eisenhower said, "initial military success might be easy … the eventual price might become far too heavy."

Almost two weeks after Nasser had addressed the crowds in Alexandria, Eden addressed the nation. In his broadcast on the BBC he conjured up one of the demons of the last war, comparing Nasser with the dictators Britain had recently faced:

> Instead of meeting us with friendship Colonel Nasser conducted a vicious propaganda campaign against this country. He has shown that he is not a man who can be trusted to keep an agreement … We all know this is how fascist governments behave, as we all remember, only too well, what the cost can be in giving in to Fascism.

Eden followed up his message to the British people with another message to Eisenhower on 5 August, grasping at what he saw as a unanimity of purpose between Washington and London: "I do not think we disagree about the primary objective: to undo what Nasser has done and set up an international regime … to ensure the freedom and security of transit through the Canal." However, at the end of his communication Eden revealed his other intention, one which he justified with the use of Cold War rhetoric, "The removal of Nasser and the installation in Egypt of a regime less hostile to the West must therefore also rank high among our objectives."

In Paris, the response to Nasser bordered on apoplectic. The French minister for foreign affairs, Christian Pineau, told a U.S. representative, "the French government takes a most serious view of the affair and links it to the seizure of the Rhineland by Hitler." Eisenhower made no such connections, describing the statements coming out of London and Paris as "based far more on emotion than on fact and logic".

A fortnight after the crisis had begun, it was already clear that Britain and France were readying themselves for a military intervention that would be regarded by their closest Cold War ally as complete folly.

## Colonialists and Fascists

De Lesseps's fame for the canal earned him many accolades. Pictured is Avenue de Lesseps in the French Gardens at Ismailia, circa 1940.

Said Pasha, whom de Lesseps convinced to help fund and provide workers for the construction of the canal.

## Suez Crisis 1956

Officers of the Lancashire Fusiliers at Kasr el Nil Barracks, Cairo, 1898. They are wearing red roses on their pith helmets to commemorate the defeat of the French at Minden on 1 August 1759.

Sudanese prisoners in chains carry the baggage of British soldiers (probably 21st Lancers) through the streets of Wadi Halfa, during Kitchener's campaign of 1898.

# 3. THE VIEW FROM THE EAST

Nearly 6,000 miles east of Washington, another leader debated how to respond to Nasser's actions. For David Ben-Gurion, an aggressive, nationalistic Egypt was a much more pressing concern, given that Egypt was on Israel's southern border.

The Israeli prime minister's short, squat stature and wispy, white hair belied a profound sense of purpose. The charismatic 70-year-old had worked tirelessly his whole life to found a national home for the Jewish people; Ben-Gurion was the Zionist statesman who had announced to the world the creation of the State of Israel in May 1948. Alongside Ben-Gurion was Israeli Chief of Staff Moshe Dayan. Born and raised in the first kibbutz – collective settlement – in Palestine, he was an unflinching personification of the ideals that birthed his homeland through the fires of war. Dayan lost an eye fighting Vichy French forces in Lebanon in 1941 and thereafter wore an eyepatch that gave him a piratical air, although decades later he would become a surprising critic of militaristic Israeli foreign policy. In 1956, both men were concerned above all with the security of their young nation.

The State of Israel was less than a decade old and its first act had been to fight for its life against a coalition of Arab armies which included Egypt. Although the 1948 war

David Ben-Gurion, the founding father of the State of Israel.

## Suez Crisis 1956

Moshe Dayan.

Raids by *fedayeen* led to violent reprisals by Israeli forces.

ended in a victory for Israel, it was not the end of the fighting. Armed struggle against Israel was taken up by Palestinian refugees who had been displaced by the conflict and who organized bands of *fedayeen* – guerrilla fighters – with aid and support from Egypt.

The loss to Israel in the war of independence was a cause of deep embarrassment in Egypt and Nasser was ardently and openly hostile to Israel. He even publicly admitted Egyptian support of the *fedayeen*, declaring in a speech in 1955,

> Egypt has decided to dispatch her heroes, the disciples of Pharaoh and the sons of Islam and they will cleanse the land of Palestine ... There will be no peace on Israel's border because we demand vengeance, and vengeance is Israel's death.

In the face of open border hostility – which Dayan responded to with violent reprisals – the Egyptian step toward the Soviets seemed another sign that Nasser genuinely was bent on bringing about Israel's 'death'.

Following the Czech arms deal, Ben-Gurion's predecessor as prime minister recorded in his diary he felt a "deep concern to our security, the likes of which I have never experienced since the days preceding the establishment of the State". Ben-Gurion thus

Israeli reprisals for *fedayeen* attacks continued long after 1956; pictured are Israeli paratroops leaving the destroyed village of Samua in Hebron in 1966, a reprisal for the killing of three Israeli soldiers.

found himself in power facing awkward odds: in 1955 Israel only had fifty jet fighters, none as good as the MiGs the Egyptians had on order. The Israelis turned to France.

In June 1956, Moshe Dayan flew to a military airfield near Paris in an Israeli Air Force transport plane painted with French insignia. He left having agreed a $100 million cash deal for French Mystère IV fighters, along with tanks and ammunition. The first tranche of arms reached Israel the night before Nasser nationalized the canal, delivered to a deserted beach near Haifa by a French amphibious landing vessel. Ben-Gurion and Dayan were waiting on the sand to meet it and after the thirty tanks, ammunition and spare parts had been unloaded, the pair boarded the ship and drank champagne with the French captain. Even before the Suez Crisis began there was an arms race in the Middle East.

War between Egypt and Israel was simply assumed to be an inevitability. The Israelis could not afford for Egypt to gain military superiority, as it was perceived that as soon as it was achieved Egypt would attack and Israeli would again be fighting for its life. One of Dayan's aides recalled following the end of the Suez Crisis:

> From [October 1955] onwards, the whole nation, and in particular the IDF [Israeli Defense Forces], was living under the threat and strain of this motto: 'there will be war in the summer of 1956.' Everyone was talking about this forthcoming war with complete certainty, as though it was just one stage in a thoroughly worked-out plan.

French-built Israeli Mystère fighter jets.

The country's prime minister phrased it more colourfully: war, Ben-Gurion said, was marching toward Israel "like an unfolding Greek drama".

Ben-Gurion's response to Nasser's seizure of the canal was to urge caution. The closure of the canal did not affect Israeli ships, as for years the Egyptians had prevented them from transiting the canal anyway; in September 1954, Israel had sent a ship down the waterway to test Egyptian resolve and the Egyptians confiscated the vessel and imprisoned the crew for three months. Access to Suez was a moot point for the Israelis, but the crisis presented an opportunity for a pre-emptive war against Egypt in which Israel could gain the upper hand. However, when Dayan pitched up with plans for an attack on Egyptian-controlled Gaza and the Sinai, Ben-Gurion told him they should "sit tight and conclude the French [arms] deal quickly, reinforce our strength, and then, at a later stage, find the right moment to strike".

It was expected that France and Britain might mount military action, although privately Ben-Gurion doubted that Britain would go to war without U.S. backing, which he did not expect would be forthcoming: "there is no hope", he remarked, "of that scoundrel Dulles supporting any daring action against the Arabs and the Russians." Ben-Gurion and Dayan still fully expected to go to war with Egypt, but not over the canal. Having been convinced of the merits of caution, Dayan agreed with his prime minister, stating, "We should not interfere in the Suez affair."

In Moscow, the reaction to the seizure of the Suez Canal was one of total surprise, as it had been in London, Paris and Washington. Egypt's ambassador in Moscow received a telling-off at the hands of the Russian foreign minister who chastised him with the words "At least you, our friends, should have consulted us", but Nasser had barely even consulted his own cabinet. Far from seeing the crisis as an opportunity for the nefarious "activities" the U.S. National Security Council insisted the Soviets were planning across the Middle East, the response of the Soviet leadership – the Politburo – was to try and avoid open confrontation with Britain and France. The first official announcement did not come out of Moscow until the end of July, when Khrushchev stated there were "no grounds for showing nervousness or alarm ... We are convinced the situation in the Suez Canal Zone will not become tense unless it is artificially aggravated."

The 62-year-old Communist Party leader came from humble origins in southwest Russia and had received little formal education. He had risen gradually through the ranks of the Communist Party, officially becoming leader following Stalin's death, before shocking his colleagues by publicly denouncing Stalin's mass murder and other crimes. Personally he was extroverted, brash and a crude joker, but when it came to foreign policy he primarily sought "peaceful coexistence" between East and West.

Like Eisenhower, Khrushchev privately viewed Nasser's action as a petulant response, suggesting the Egyptian leader was "only playing, trying to extract from the West a larger sum [of money for the Aswan dam]". While Khrushchev led the Communist Party, the official head of state of the Soviet Union was Premier Nikolai Bulganin. He was Khrushchev's ally and the two men worked together and generally travelled

Soviet leader Khrushchev with U.S. Vice-President Nixon.

overseas side by side; they were irreverently referred to by one British press outlet as "the B and K show". At the start of August, when the U.S. ambassador to Moscow met with Bulganin, the Russian premier pointed out the remarkable fact that "there seemed to be between the United States and the Soviet Union a common position that both felt this matter must be settled by peaceful means".

The two great Cold War powers who were engaged in an ideological, technical and, in parts of the globe, violent struggle for supremacy were in agreement: Nasser's shutting of Suez was not worth going to war over.

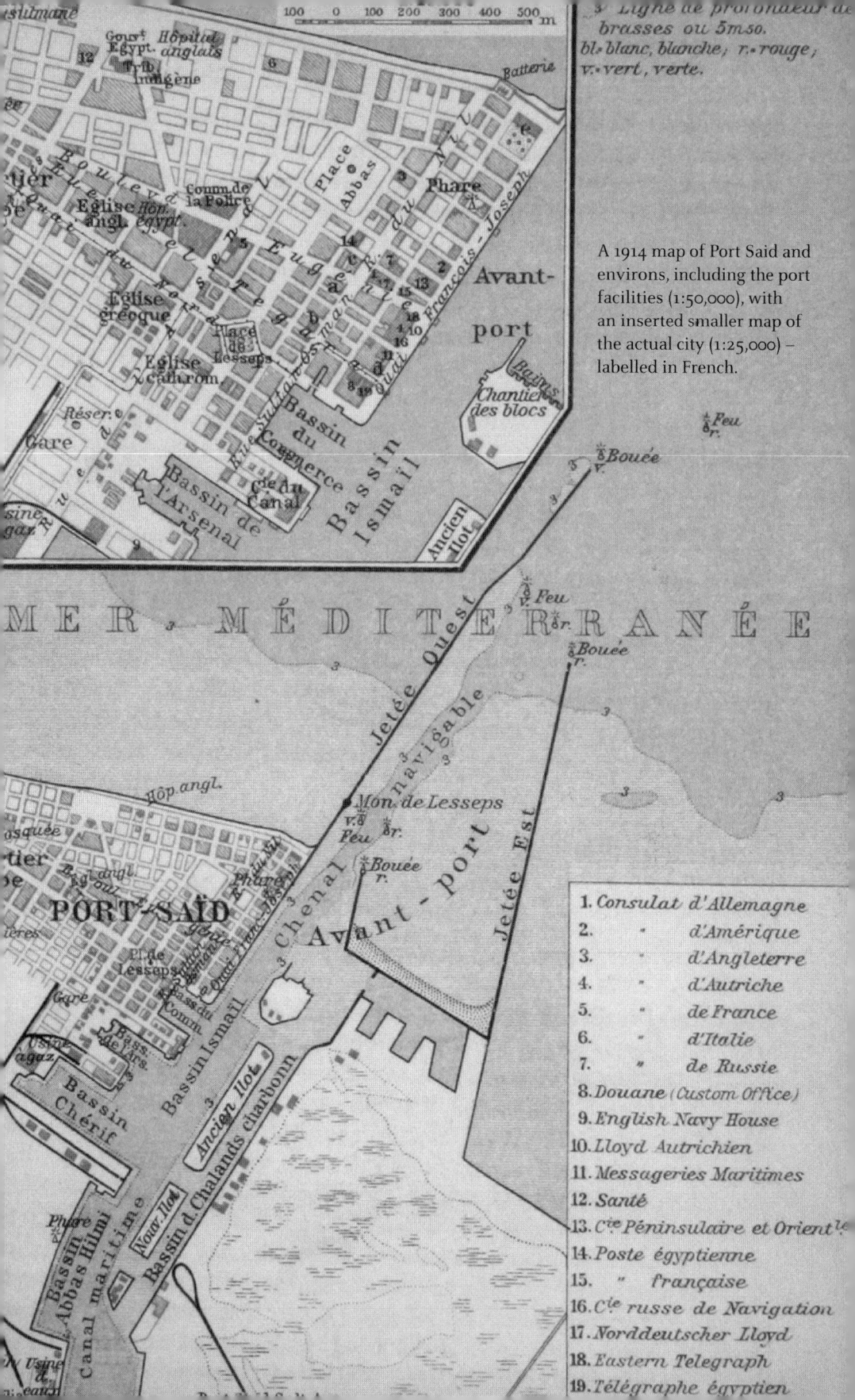

A 1914 map of Port Said and environs, including the port facilities (1:50,000), with an inserted smaller map of the actual city (1:25,000) – labelled in French.

Suez Crisis 1956

Prince Farouk Street, Port Said, February 1942.

Local Arab men and boys in one of the bustling side alleys of downtown Cairo, 1942.

# 4. SATISFACTION

It has become fashionable to present the Suez Crisis as an unnecessary war that the French and British, and in particular Anthony Eden, were determined to start regardless of international opinion or strategic sense. However, in August 1956 both the British and the French were open to non-military solutions.

There was no doubt about the perceived gravity of the seizure of the canal in Britain: as the under-secretary of state for foreign affairs proclaimed in rather colonialist language at the start of the crisis, "in two years' time Nasser will have deprived us of our oil, the sterling area falling apart ... [there will be] unemployment and unrest in the UK and our standard of living reduced to that of [the] Yugoslavs or the Egyptians." But it would be wrong to suggest that the U.S. acquiesced to Nasser's action. The president had already declared that Nasser should be made to "disgorge his theft" and, in a letter to Eden, Eisenhower noted:

> We have two problems, the first of which is the assurance of permanent and efficient operation of the Canal. The second is to see that Nasser shall not grow as a menace to peace and the vital interests of the West. The first is the most important and must not be resolved in such a way as to make the second more difficult.

The French were also in agreement with the American position at the start of August, when Pineau met with Dulles. The French foreign minister told his opposite number, "We agree, however, that we should first try other means." Pineau was, however, very clear what the alternative was. He told Dulles the French intended to propose to Nasser international management of the canal, adding darkly,

> If he accepts it, we will have satisfaction. If he does not, we will intervene with the British. If the Americans do not join this intervention, we would expect of them that they would take a position such that it would convince the Russians not to intervene.

In August 1956, there was a window of opportunity for a peaceful resolution to the Suez Crisis.

What was proposed was a multinational maritime conference in London to discuss a British, French and American plan to establish international authority to operate the canal in accordance with prior agreements of access, while also ensuring Egypt received an "equitable return".

Twenty-four governments were invited, including the Russians, who responded to their invitation through a statement published in *Pravda* on 10 August. They highlighted the fact that Nasser had already promised to allow freedom of navigation through the canal (for everyone except the Israelis), asserting the conference "cannot in any way be regarded, either in its composition or in character and purposes, as an international meeting authorized to take any decisions whatever on the Suez Canal". A Russian delegation came to London anyway, but insisted it didn't commit them to anything, or make the outcome legitimate.

Only two countries turned down their invitations to attend: Greece and Egypt. Remarkably, Nasser had considered attending the London conference in person. His first instinct was to go and he had to be talked out of it by his Cabinet; one told Nasser that Egypt should not be a "mere invitee". After several days of consideration, Nasser came round, concluding that "the Egyptian case would not even be considered", claiming that the agenda had already been fixed and the decisions already made. Any possibility of his attending was then immediately scuppered when Eden made his BBC televised address, comparing Nasser to the Fascists Britain had fought in the war and condemning him as "not a man who can be trusted to keep an agreement".

The first London conference opened on 16 August. That night, Dulles reported back to Eisenhower, "The atmosphere on the whole is much more composed than two weeks ago." Eden was optimistic that the conference might result in what had always been his preferred outcome: international ownership of the canal that protected traffic, but saved the British government the bill. He wrote to Churchill after the first couple of days of deliberations, "We are only at the beginning, but there are some encouraging elements. Most important of all the Americans seem very firmly lined up with us on internationalism." He also confirmed "[military] Preparations about which I spoke to you are going forward with some modifications, which should lead to a simplification of our plan should the need arise." The impression of strong U.S. support was entirely created by Dulles, whose speech proposing the solution backed by Britain and France came across as almost a recitation of their case, including the assertion "The international confidence which rested upon the convention of 1866 with the Suez Canal Company and the treaty of 1888 has been grievously assaulted."

Almost from the outset, the conference appeared to be hurtling down the tracks to a predetermined conclusion. As British publication *The Spectator* explained to its readers on the first day of meetings:

> In the eyes of most countries Egypt has done nothing so very wrong by her nationalization of the Suez Canal, while Britain and France have managed to give their actions an appearance of aggression ... Our position there will be a weak one. Even though there may be a majority for internationalization of the Canal, there will certainly be no majority for forcing this on Egypt.

Pursuing a diplomatic solution while preparing for military action seemed logical to Eden, but appeared a rather obvious ploy in foreign capitals. As the London

Eisenhower and Dulles meeting on 14 August 1956.

conference was ending, the British ambassador in Moscow was summoned to see an angry Khrushchev, who told him:

> Even if you have interests, do you need to mobilize armies and threaten war to protect them? Don't forget that if a war starts because of what you are doing, all our sympathies will be with Egypt. A war of Egypt against Britain would be a sacred war, and if my son came to me, and asked me if he ought to volunteer to fight against Britain, I would tell him he most certainly should do so.

In case the message was not clear enough, *Pravda* published shortly afterwards:

> It is clear that in the event of a colonialist attack upon Egypt, the war of the Egyptian people against the foreign enslavers would be a just war of liberation. Therefore, Egypt would have the warm sympathy and active support of the whole of progressive mankind.

In the meantime, the "foreign enslavers" had agreed upon a proposal for the canal's future. Unsurprisingly it was the one backed by Britain and France and in total eighteen of the twenty-two nations who had attended the conference. Australian Prime Minister Robert Menzies was tasked with going to Cairo to sell it to Nasser. In hindsight, he was potentially the wrong candidate; he may have been of Commonwealth stock, but he came across as just another Englishman in a suit, who described Nasser after their meeting as "obviously the master of his government, but with some marks of immaturity and inevitable lack of experience". During his meeting to pitch the peaceful solution to the crisis he rather

## Suez Crisis 1956

Israeli children and nannies leave their bomb shelter during the build-up to the Suez Crisis.

unpeacefully told Nasser it would "be a mistake for you to exclude the possibility of force [being used against Egypt]". Rather accurately, Nasser slammed the whole thing as "collective colonialism" and rejected the proposals of the conference, telling a U.S. diplomat he was "not ready to welcome a man who acts like an Australian mule which Eden has sent, to scare me".

There was still no legal basis for the use of force, but that was not deterring preparations. British- and French-flagged vessels using the canal were ordered to refuse to pay transit fees, largely in the hope that the Egyptians would react. As one Foreign Office official noted, "We shall need any luck in the way of provocation from Colonel Nasser and I would suggest that the concerted denial of canal dues should ... have a high priority." Given that British vessels accounted for 80 per cent of traffic on the canal, the move was intended to make the canal unprofitable for Egypt.

The French had also joined the British in putting together logistical preparations required for military action. On 26 August, French paratroopers arrived in Cyprus while the French also arranged the relocation of 120 aircraft to airfields on the island. The first window for a peaceful resolution of the Suez Crisis had slammed shut.

*Satisfaction*

Heavily laden southbound dhows on the Suez Canal. Passengers and livestock await the Kantara ferry at the El Kantara wharf.

President Nasser raises the Egyptian flag over the local naval headquarters at Port Said in celebration of the British military withdrawal from the canal zone a few days prior, 18 June 1956.

## Suez Crisis 1956

Nasser with his children, May 1956. Five months later on Abdul's fifth birthday (pictured far right), Israel invaded the Sinai.

Nasser and Khrushchev pictured at the diverting of the Nile for construction of the Aswan dam.

# 5. A SWIM FROM MALTA

It was a mirthless irony not entirely lost on British military logistics wizards that they were now planning how to transport thousands of soldiers to attack the Suez Canal, when less than six months previously they had been carefully planning how to evacuate thousands soldiers from the same place. The problem, as Eden admitted years later in his memoirs, was one of logistics. "Unless we could fly all the forces needed, they had to swim. The nearest place from which to swim was Malta, a thousand miles away."

The flying option was an attractive notion: an elegant and seemingly simple military solution that had lured generals for decades since the invention and first deployment of airborne troops. However, the Second World War disasters of the airborne invasion of Crete and the catastrophe at Arnhem had proved beyond doubt that insufficiently supported paratroops were no match for well-equipped ground forces. Besides, the British

The sailing of the naval task force from Malta was impossible to keep secret; from left: HMS *Eagle*, *Bulwark* and *Albion*.

and French combined did not possess enough paratroops to retake Suez unaided and deal a telling blow to Nasser, and not all of the ones they had were even ready; British paratroops stationed in Cyprus had spent a year chasing Greek partisans in the Troodos mountains and had neglected to do any parachute training. The problem was compounded by the fact that there were too few transport aircraft to hand, so Eden's musings on the night of 26 July that British paratroops could descend from the sky at key points along the canal to give Nasser a swift and salutary lesson in power politics never came to anything. At least some soldiers would have to "swim", as Eden phrased it, which meant that it would be almost impossible to secretly build up and sail an armada to Suez without almost half the world being aware of the fact.

Military planning had started immediately after Nasser nationalized the canal and the first outline for the operation, put together on 31 July, proposed a Royal Marine amphibious assault, combined with an attack by paratroops flown from Cyprus. Infantry and armour would set out by sea and mount an amphibious landing at Port Said harbour. The entire operation would be supported by RAF Valiant and Canberra bombers, as well as carrier-borne aircraft from the Mediterranean Fleet. The idea of simply trying to force Nasser to capitulate through airstrikes was considered, but "unseating the present Egyptian government by bombing alone" was, it was concluded, an unlikely prospect. Not to be deterred, the air minister, Nigel Birch, entirely seriously proposed that Nasser might be more amenable if rumours were spread that an atom bomb might be dropped on the cities of Cairo or Alexandria.

The plan proposed by the Joint Staff was not universally well received. Eden's chancellor, Harold Macmillan, was one of the more hawkish members of the Cabinet, and the idea of an operation focused on the canal seemed to him to be missing the point. "The object of the exercise," he wrote in early August, "is surely to bring about the fall of Nasser and create a government in Egypt which will work satisfactorily with us." The most acceptable use of force would be to coerce Nasser into internationalizing the canal, but Eden and his chancellor also wanted Nasser gone. There was little nuanced thought about who might replace Nasser if he were successfully removed. As one CIA agent in the region later recalled, they had no information, nor did their contacts in MI6, as to who might replace Nasser if he was toppled, but British ministers

> didn't seem to care. They thought they should get rid of Nasser, hang the practical consequences, just to show the world that an upstart like him couldn't get away with so ostentatiously twisting the lion's tail.

The broader aim of bringing down Nasser resulted in an alternative military solution being drawn up, which began with three days of airstrikes followed by a landing at Alexandria and an advance toward the canal itself via Cairo. The leading British general explained the logic of the diversion to the Egyptian capital as, "the Egyptians would be forced either to capitulate or to stand and fight us ... where their army would be annihilated".

Eden and a select group of ministers gave the go-ahead for the plan on 10 August and Operation *Musketeer* was put in motion. But Eden would have to wait. The earliest date the planners reckoned it could start was 15 September, and even then they were cutting corners. While military logisticians worked their slide rules, the Parachute Brigade Group in Cyprus was recalled to England to practise jumping out of aeroplanes.

The French contribution to *Musketeer* was to offer 2,000 paratroops, additional land forces and air power, although British high command were extremely reticent to share their plans with the French. The start date of 15 September was about two weeks later than the French had hoped for and two members of the French chiefs of staff pitched up in London to offer whatever they could to speed things up. The typical British attitude to their eager allies was summed up by Foreign Secretary Selwyn Lloyd's response to the French offer, in which he explained that, as he comprehended it, the real limiting factor was a lack of assault craft "of which I understand the French have none".

Selwyn Lloyd was an unspectacular politician who had been elected an MP after serving as an infantry staff officer in the war. When he was asked to join the Foreign Office by the then prime minister Winston Churchill he was flabbergasted. He told Churchill he thought there must have been a mistake, adding, "I do not speak any foreign language. Except in war, I have never visited any foreign country. I do not like foreigners." His protestations were entirely disregarded by Churchill, who told Lloyd, "Young man, these all seem to me to be positive advantages."

Lloyd became foreign secretary shortly after Eden assumed the premiership. He was the archetypal unassuming politician, who arrived at his station by being a safe pair of hands and was terribly suited to being foreign secretary. In one respect, Lloyd was perhaps Eden's ideal foreign secretary as he could be relied upon to do as he was told. As one civil servant later noted, Lloyd was "a modest man and was not very confident in his own judgement".

There were other issues with the planned attack, namely the unquantifiable factor of Soviet-made weaponry. The aircraft and tanks had been delivered, but it was reliably assessed that their Egyptian operators were not yet up to speed on their new equipment. In a personal note to Eden, Churchill stressed his concern over the delay to a military operation, pointing out that because of the delay, "it should be possible for at least 1,000 Russian and similar volunteers to take over the cream of the Egyptian aircraft and tanks". Russian-made fighters flown by inexperienced Egyptian pilots were a minor headache compared to the prospect of MiGs flown by battle-hardened Soviet aces masquerading as Egyptians. The solution would be to destroy as much as possible of the Egyptian Air Force on the ground, a plan which would utilize the state-of-the-art Canberra bomber.

The nuclear-capable Canberra had been introduced in 1951 as a high-altitude, high-speed bomber – a modern jet that replaced the much-loved de Havilland Mosquito in RAF service. The Canberra possessed a unique, pinpoint bombing technology that triangulated the aircraft's position using radio beacons, but which was completely useless over the Eastern Mediterranean. The result was that the pilots and bomb aimers of one of the world's

The Marines had to practise landing alongside tanks ahead of the operation to take Port Said.

most sophisticated aircraft found they would have to revert to World-War-II-style tactics if they were to land their bombs on the Egyptian airfields they would be targeting, tactics they would have to re-learn. It was another unforeseen complication.

The military preparations carried on apace during the first London conference – as Eden admitted in his note to Churchill – which came across at the very least as contradictory. French enthusiasm for a diplomatic solution never matched that across the Channel and a senior British civil servant felt the need to impress upon the French ahead of the discussions that the British were taking it seriously, writing, "We do not regard the London conference as a formality ... to be observed before we can proceed to effective action."

By the end of August, French paratroops and aircraft had been relocated to Cyprus and HMS *Ark Royal*, originally the only aircraft carrier in the Mediterranean Fleet, had been joined by five more. In Malta, the Amphibious Warfare Squadron was readying its tank landing vessels, although in the process it was discovered that the Royal Marines had not practised an amphibious landing with tanks in over a year.

Regardless of such hiccups, *Musketeer* was still on schedule. When Australian Prime Minister Menzies arrived in Cairo to warn Nasser that he should not "exclude the possibility of force" if he refused to accept the London conference plan of international control of the canal, it seemed in some quarters that the diplomacy was little more than a merry dance to mark time until Britain and France had marshalled their armies.

# 6. AN INVITATION

On 1 September Israeli Prime Minister David Ben-Gurion received an urgent message from Paris. French officials had told an Israeli representative they were preparing for war against Nasser alongside Britain and wanted to inquire whether the Israelis would like to join in a week after it started. Moshe Dayan, on hearing the idea, recorded in his diary,

> If indeed Britain and France capture the Suez Canal and restore its international status by force of arms, the political implications for us will be of the highest importance. Not only will the Canal be open (I hope) to Israeli shipping, but Britain will be engaged in a military conflict with Egypt over interests which serve us too.

Given that the Israelis were anticipating having to go to war with Egypt anyway, doing so with a guarantee of swift victory was an attractive proposition. Ben-Gurion's response was "in principle, we are willing to cooperate" and it was quickly communicated back to the French. Following Nasser's outright rejection of the proposals arising from the London conference the position in Paris seemed to have hardened. Pineau told the Israeli ambassador, "there was no other way out except Nasser's surrender or war." Ben-Gurion still doubted whether Eden in particular would actually go through with the threat of military action and was perplexed by the situation that had developed six weeks after Nasser had taken the canal, admitting it was "hard to accept that two governments of European powers would make laughing stocks of themselves by threatening to dispatch armies, navies and air forces [and] then submit to the Egyptian dictator".

As Ben-Gurion digested the proposal from Paris, Eden received a salutary communication from the White House. In it, Eisenhower told Eden "American public opinion" rejected the use of force against Nasser. He added a caution that military action "might cause a serious misunderstanding between our two countries", pointing out that public opinion "seems to think that the United Nations was formed to prevent this very thing".

The timing was notable. At the end of August, Eisenhower had received his rapturous second nomination for re-election at the Republican Party convention and suddenly the scheduled presidential election in November 1956 loomed large. In reply, Eden was careful with his words, still keeping diplomacy open but stating, "we must have some immediate alternative which will show that Nasser is not going to get his way." He painted the Suez Crisis in a Cold War context, insisting that they could not wait "until this country and all Western Europe are held to ransom by Egypt acting at Russia's behest".

Even though the first diplomatic effort had failed, the Americans proposed a potential alternative. Dulles's bright idea was that instead of the canal being owned and run by the British and French with the Egyptians getting payment, the canal could be officially owned by Egypt but still run by the international powers. Eisenhower was not entirely convinced by the Dulles idea, which would take control of toll collection away from the Egyptians, but he encouraged his secretary of state to pursue it as a way of stalling a war. It seemed it might be a path to a diplomatic settlement that would allow Egypt to claim a victory and also persuade the British and French to stand down their invasion plans. Even if it failed, the protracted negotiations would at least take up significant time. Eisenhower told Dulles the key thing was "not to make any mistakes in a hurry".

The second proposed diplomatic solution would recognize Egypt as being in charge of the canal but leave the running of the waterway to an international Suez Canal Users' Association (SCUA). In reality it was little more than a plan pulled out of a hat and hastily scribbled down, with Dulles admitting, "Every day that goes by … is gain … I don't know anything to do but keep improvising."

Dulles's "improvising" led to the scheduling of a second conference in London starting on 19 September, but not everyone was on the same page. Eden presented the SCUA idea to Parliament as a method of retaking control of the management of maritime traffic and toll collection from the Egyptians, adding that if Nasser failed to cooperate the next port of call would be the UN, followed by recourse to "other means". Eden was already half-forming in the back of his mind the unbecoming notion that Dulles's enthusiasm for the users' association was more motivated by a desire for delay than diplomacy. He confided in a letter to his friend and predecessor Churchill:

> I am not very happy with the way things are developing here, but we are struggling hard to keep a firm and united front in these critical weeks … Foster [Dulles] assures me that the U.S. is as determined to deal with Nasser as we are, but I fear he has a mental caveat about November 6th [polling day in the U.S.].

On 11 September, Eden, British Foreign Secretary Selwyn Lloyd and his French opposite number Pineau met at 10 Downing Street. Pineau was convinced the entire SCUA idea was little more than stalling tactic. He told Eden and Lloyd:

> We are really wasting our time talking to the Americans … they will never authorize any action likely to provoke the fall of Nasser, at any rate until after the American elections … our two countries should now go firmly ahead on our chosen path.

Eden did not disagree, but there seemed to be sense in at least trying Dulles's proposal. The meeting ended in the agreement that the British and French would support the idea, but that if it failed they would go to the UN for backing. In truth, Dulles was prevaricating and CIA field officers in the region began to jokingly refer to SCUA" as "SKREWYA" with 'you' being the British and the French.

The day before the second London conference opened, Moshe Dayan secretly flew to Paris. The French were losing confidence in Eden's determination for military action and the defence minister told the Israelis that, personally, he thought "other partners have to be found for war against Nasser". The French theory was that there were now different timetables for war: an American timetable, which might basically never happen, the British timetable which would be months of more fruitless diplomacy and the French timetable, which was for action now. When they were put to Ben-Gurion he stated, "It is the French timetable that is most to our liking. If they move out at a time which is convenient to them, we shall stand by them to the best of our ability."

The French wish was simple: "immediate action against Nasser, bearing in mind not only the Suez situation, but also developments in North Africa." It gave away the other reason the French were angry at Nasser: Algeria.

The country of Algeria in North Africa had been a French *department* since 1830, but had descended into violence in 1954. Algeria was not simply a colony that France was reluctant to part with: as a *department* it was officially part of France and Guy Mollet and Pineau had every intention of it staying that way.

By early 1956 there were 200,000 French troops in the country fighting against the Front de libération nationale (FLN) which was demanding independence. The struggle in majority Muslim Algeria would be bitter and brutal, but in 1956 the French concern was that the Algerian rebels were receiving aid from Egypt. Radio Cairo, which so annoyed Eden with its anti-British broadcasts, was noisily voicing support for the FLN and its cause. When Pineau confronted Nasser directly on the issue during a flying visit to Egypt in March 1956, Nasser gave him his "word of honour as a soldier" that Egypt was not sponsoring the Algerian rebels, but the assumption

French Prime Minister Guy Mollet was 51 when the Suez Crisis erupted. The former German prisoner of war had been premier for only five months when Nasser nationalized the canal.

was it was probably a lie, especially given Nasser's "theft" of the canal. The French directly linked the Suez Crisis to the escalating war in Algeria: as Pineau noted after a meeting with Selwyn Lloyd:

> If the action of Egypt remains without a response, it would be useless to continue the struggle in Algeria ... I recalled the warnings that Hitler had provided to the democracies of which none of our three countries had taken into account. This lesson should inspire our action.

The bellicose attitude of the French was not going unnoticed. On 11 September, while Eden met with Pineau at Downing Street, two Politburo members cornered the French ambassador in Moscow. "Do you really want to make war on Egypt?" they inquired, "Haven't you [had] enough of war in Algeria?" Their question came with a prophecy that if France took military action "All the Arab World will stand against you. The war will be without end. You will wind up in a quagmire." The ambassador was sanguine in the face of the threat however and later that day communicated to Paris how he thought the Russians would respond: they would send weapons, help recruit foreign volunteer fighters and maybe send military advisers, but they would not intervene as long as the U.S. kept out of it.

Captured FLN fighters in Algeria.

*An Invitation*

Selwyn Lloyd (far left) as Foreign Secretary in 1960, seen here with other European foreign ministers.

Christian Pineau, seen here in June 1945 as the French minister of supplies. Having served in The Resistance, he quickly rose through the ranks of government.

DER
SUÊS-KANAL
Maßstab 1:500.000
Kilometer
Ehemal. Ballâh-Seen
El-Ferdân
Bir Abu 'Arâk
Dünen von El-Ferdân
El-Gisr
durchschnittl. 16m Seehöhe
Bir Magdal
ISMAÏLIYE
Timsâh-See
Hyänen-Plateau
Bir el-Fauar
Schich Hanaidik
Tusun
Bir Murra
Serapeum
Maritimer Kanal
El-'Ambek
Grosses Bassin
Bittere Seen
Leuchtturm
Kleines Bassin
Gebel Geneffe oder Gebel Ahmed Taher
Stat. Geneffe
Gebel Schalûf et-Terrâbe
Schalûf et-Terrâbe
Taverniera-Tal
Fort Agerud
Derb el-Hagg
Wadi Suês
Bir Sues
'Atâka-Ebene
SUES
Port Ibrahim
Gebel 'Atâka
Arsinoë
Yumm el-Gemile, Tanitische Mündung
PORT SAÏD
Menzale-See
Kôm Rumâde
Trocken gelegter Seeboden
Pelusischer Nil-Arm
Tell esch-Scherig
El-Kantara
Bir Heleli
Ehemal. Ballâh-Seen

# 7. TO THE UNITED NATIONS

The second London conference began on 19 September in a febrile atmosphere. Four days before, the Suez Canal Company's non-Egyptian pilots responsible for guiding vessels down the narrow waterway left their posts at the encouragement of their employer. Of the 201 company pilots, only forty were Egyptian and at the moment of the walkout five of them were on holiday. Eden's Cabinet had openly discussed the hope that the pilots' departure would see the canal turn into a chaotic queue of ships and Selwyn Lloyd faced questions in Parliament on whether their departure had been encouraged by the government; the accusation was not entirely without basis as the very day the pilots left their posts a suspiciously long line of fifty, mostly British-flagged, ships, arrived at Port Said to transit the canal. Instead of descending into disorder, the canal continued to run smoothly, as pilots from Egypt, the Soviet Union and India stepped in to help ships navigate safely, taking them one by one the length of the waterway. The Suez Canal was now entirely in Egyptian hands, but traffic was still sailing freely through it. Nasser was triumphant and bestowed honours on all the Egyptian pilots who worked long hours to prove the Western governments wrong. It was a watershed moment.

The Soviets refused to attend the second London conference, branding it a "provocation" to engineer a case for military action. This was unfair on Dulles, who had intended the conference to be obfuscation which would make military action more difficult. To no one's surprise, the second London conference ended with an agreement on the basic premise of SCUA, but the parties that might have objected were not present.

The French were reluctant signatories and were mainly going along with the SCUA idea because securing British military assistance seemed to require the obvious exhausting of all diplomatic options. Pineau circulated a note to the British and American ambassadors after the conference, which insisted that France intended to retain its "freedom of action". The French press was in a less charitable mood, particularly towards the Americans. The conspiracy theory was that Eisenhower was appeasing the Hitler of the Middle East to bring an end to French control of Algeria and open the country up to U.S. oil companies. It was laughable, but it demonstrated the level of hawkish opinion that persisted in Paris. As the editor of *Le Figaro* phrased it, "If the Suez Crisis has taken a bad turn, it is because the support of our American friends has been completely denied to us from the beginning."

After exploring and agreeing to Dulles's bright idea, Eden now saw it for what it was. The U.S. secretary of state, Eden remarked, was "stringing us along at least until polling day". Five days after the end of the SCUA conference, Eden and Lloyd travelled to Paris. They met the French to discuss the next step: taking the Suez Crisis to the UN Security Council.

## Suez Crisis 1956

Recourse to the United Nations was a perfectly logical move for Eden. The British prime minister had been one of the early proponents of the organization and at one point had been touted a potential first secretary-general. The long-running fallout from the Suez Crisis has created a false impression of Eden as a nationalist hardliner, but for most of his political career Eden was an ardent internationalist. Only two years previously, Eden had defied everyone's expectations and secured a peace agreement to halt the deterioration of the French government's war in Indochina, spending weeks encouraging and cajoling the French, Russians, Vietnamese and Chinese into a settlement.

At the time it had been U.S. Secretary of State Dulles who had been pushing for an escalation of the conflict, which could potentially have triggered a third world war. By taking the Suez Crisis to the UN, Eden could obtain international moral support for any action that might follow. Pineau was sceptical, describing the UN as having the power of "suspensive action", but Eden wished to try. He was still wary, noting later "means had to be found to prevent the endless circumlocutions and eventual disregard which usually befell resolutions coming before the [Security] Council". The plan was to put

Eden's performance at the Geneva Conference two years previously had been widely praised for preventing a war in Indochina. The *Daily Mirror* had named him 'politician of the year'.

forward a resolution seeking support for an internationally run waterway, although it was expected that the Russians would veto it.

Mollet and Pineau were, Eden recalled, "sceptical about the United Nations ... the French favoured action at an early date." Eden expressed sympathy, but he and Lloyd insisted they should give the UN Security Council the opportunity of "maintaining international agreements", although he added, "If necessary we would be prepared to use whatever steps, including force, that might be needed to re-establish respect for these obligations." Publicly, he was only marginally less strident, telling journalists at Le Bourget airport as he and Lloyd returned to London:

> This crisis ... has not only endangered the economic interests of many nations, but has constituted an attack on the traditional respect of treaties. This was the lesson before the [Second World] war, and is also one today.

A few days ahead of the start of the UN debate, Dulles gave a press conference in which he stated that the U.S. had to play "a somewhat independent role" in the "shift from colonialism to independence". It was hardly reassuring language for the British and the French to hear. Even less reassuring was Dulles's assertion in answer to a question that the SCUA proposals were never intended to have any 'teeth', already holing below the waterline the plan to use a UN Security Council resolution as the stick to force the London conference proposals on Egypt; Eden subsequently complained to the French ambassador that it seemed simply "the latest in a series of surprises which the American Secretary of State has reserved for us". Privately, Eden saw it as rank hypocrisy:

> The dispute over Nasser's seizure of the canal had, of course, nothing to do with colonialism, but was concerned with international rights. If the United States had to defend their treaty rights in the Panama Canal, they would not regard such action as colonialism.

Eden was not the only leader involved in the crisis who had considered what role the UN might play. Nasser had even debated going to the UN with a proposal to replace the 1888 canal treaty, on the basis that it infringed Egypt's sovereignty because it charged the non-Egyptian signatories with "watching over its execution". However, following the second London conference, Nasser explored other options. Egypt's ambassador to the U.S. met with a State Department diplomat in late September and presented a more flexible side to the Egyptian position. He stated Egypt's "desire to create a negotiating process", the goal of which would be "a solution which guarantees Egypt's rights and sovereignty while guaranteeing also free passage in the Canal, instead of creating a situation predicated on attacks and aggression".

As all parties headed to New York, there was a surprising but slim chance that a diplomatic solution might still be achievable, despite all the rhetoric. The question was whether the British and French would consent to any outcome that would give Nasser an opportunity to claim a victory. As one U.S. diplomat admitted in private discussions with Egyptian representatives – a comment which was immediately sent on to Nasser in Cairo – "the difficulty in solving it [the crisis] derives from Britain and France's fear for their prestige".

Egypt's foreign minister, Mahmoud Fawsi, represented the country at the UN when the debate got underway in the first week of October. The 56-year-old lawyer and linguist was privately reassured by the secretary-general of the UN that the British, or at least Foreign Secretary Lloyd, were genuinely interested in a diplomatic solution "despite the appearance to the contrary".

Dag Hammarskjöld, Secretary-General of the UN in 1956.

With Nasser's blessing, Fawsi began exploring an alternative to the London conference solutions which would "protect Egypt's sovereignty and the interests of the canal users". The idea was a six-nation committee comprised of the four "Great Powers" plus Egypt and India, although Nasser left it up to Fawsi's discretion to reveal how much the Egyptians were willing to compromise. The idea was privately backed by the Russians, while publicly they deployed their long-nurtured distrust of the UN to criticize the British and French. The Soviet foreign minister pointedly remarked

> Could it be that the ruling circles planned to reply to public demands for a peaceful settlement: "You have urged us to appeal to the UN. We have done so, but, as you see, it is powerless ... Egypt is guilty. Crucify it!"?

Remarkably, the deliberations at the UN that began in early October would come within sight of a peaceful, diplomatic solution.

The second London conference and the referral to the UN significantly delayed the original invasion plans. 15 September had come and gone. First, the start date for *Musketeer* was pushed to 25 September, then 1 October and then the plan changed. The direct assault on Alexandria and Cairo "appeared less and less adapted to the international situation", effectively an admission that a full-on invasion would look like what it was: simply an excuse to take out Nasser, Instead, the military plans were reworked to focus on the canal. The disgruntled general commanding the French land forces remarked, "Thus, after one month of studies and preparations, we came back to square one."

The intention was now that the canal would be secured at Port Said and then land forces would drive up its entire length, the British on one side and the French on the other. But *Musketeer* would not be put into motion while discussions continued at the UN.

Pineau, Lloyd and Fawsi met in the New York office of the UN secretary-general on the morning of 12 October. Fawsi was clear that Egypt was open to negotiation, but Pineau insisted that the starting point for any discussion had to be full international control of the canal and would not be moved. International control was also wrapped up in the British and French resolution and Pineau telegrammed Paris to assure his colleagues that it would be vetoed by the Soviets. He added that result "would be a tolerable outcome for France".

After banging heads with Pineau, Fawsi met with Dulles the same afternoon. The U.S. secretary of state was unequivocal in where the primary obstruction lay. "France," Dulles told Fawsi, "was trying to sabotage the agreement and enter into battle over the Suez Canal."

# 8. CASUS BELLI

French patience was running out. At the start of October Pineau had remarked: "We must go forward, but it remains to convince the English." The French were already taking practical steps and between 30 September and 1 October held another series of meetings with the Israelis, who were invited to discussions in Paris. This time Moshe Dayan was accompanied by the Israeli foreign minister, Golda Meir.

Golda Meir would go on to become Israel's first female prime minister, but in 1956 the 58-year-old, Ukrainian-born founding mother of the State of Israel was the new nation's hard-nosed overseas representative. At first glance she resembled a chain-smoking *babushka*, but any political operative who held to that notion was in for nasty shock; Golda Meir was the first female politician to be given the title 'Iron Lady'.

When they met Pineau opened the discussions. He stated that the French government had decided to use military force against Nasser and that an attack should be undertaken in October, before rougher seas in the Mediterranean hampered the operation and so that action did not directly clash with the presidential elections in the U.S.. Then came the bombshell. Would the Israelis, Pineau asked, be interested in joining the French in a military operation if the British dropped out? Without the British, the chances of a simple

Golda Meir.

victory were drastically diminished: French and British logistics were already entangled and if British-owned airfields in Cyprus were not available then French aircraft would have to fly sorties from Israel. The French were also concerned that their ground-attack aircraft were significantly inferior to the Royal Air Force's Canberra bomber, which would be a key asset for destroying the Egyptian Air Force on the ground. Without British assistance the military mission became more difficult and it opened up the possibility that cities in Israel could come under sustained bombing. Golda Meir grilled Pineau for several minutes, demanding to know what the chances were of the U.S. intervening militarily or imposing economic sanctions against Israel. Pineau was adamant the U.S. would not go to war and insisted that if the military campaign started before the elections on 6 November, Eisenhower would not want to take action against Israel for fear of alienating the Jewish vote in the States.

Dayan then presented his plans for an Israeli attack across the Sinai Desert, which impressed the French listeners, at the same time putting in a request for an additional 100 French tanks. His request was accepted. Within a week of the Israeli delegation flying home, the French began deploying a squadron of Mystère jet fighters to Israel, basing them at Ramat-David air base near Haifa, while a squadron of fighter bombers were transferred to Tel Aviv. It was a powerful statement of intent designed to assuage Israeli concerns that by going to war alongside France they would invite the bombing of Israeli cities. Three shiploads of arms – delivered ahead of payment – then left Toulin with Dayan's 100 extra tanks, plus 200 armoured half-tracks along with ammunition and fuel. The British were kept entirely in the dark.

In New York, the negotiations at the UN continued throughout October. Pineau had claimed when the debate began in the Security Council that "If we [France and Britain] had been acting with aggressive intent we would not have shown the patience we have shown ever since 26 July [when Nasser nationalized the canal]." It was a nice notion, but of course the only reason for the delay was military logistics and the British insistence on exhausting diplomacy. The French foreign secretary, who like Dulles and Lloyd, seemed to be spending half his time flying around the world, had been obdurate in talks with the Egyptians. Lloyd recalled:

> In the first three days of the private talks he appeared utterly unreasonable. He came late, went early, made difficulties about long meetings and spent considerable time at the beginning of some of the meetings arguing.

To even the casual observer, Dulles's admission to Fawsi that the French wanted a war seemed entirely accurate. The American did have a moment of regret over his withdrawal of U.S. support for the Aswan Dam which had triggered the crisis, confiding in Fawsi that he had never meant to insult Egypt, or to damage the country's economy. It was not Dulles's fault the crisis had happened, but he appeared at least repentant for his role in motivating Nasser to act.

Lloyd pressed on. Fawsi agreed in outline to 'six principles' over the canal's operation, which included free transit without discrimination, agreement between Egypt and the users on tolls and charges, the allocation of a fair amount of dues for development, arbitration to settle disputes, respect for Egypt's sovereignty and insulation of the canal from politics. He also agreed to compensating Suez Canal Company shareholders, as Nasser had promised, and to a form of cooperation with a users' association for the canal. Dulles encouraged Fawsi along before the chairman of the World Bank then met with Fawsi and intimated that if the Suez Crisis were solved amicably, Egypt might still get assistance with the Aswan Dam. Pineau was in favour of the principles but still adamantly insisted that the resolution for voting at the Security Council should include a follow-up, mandating separate, non-Egyptian international control of the canal. Lloyd, who was under strict instructions to demonstrate "solidarity" with the French had to go along.

When news of agreement between the three sides over the six principles reached Eisenhower, he went on television and announced "gratifying" progress had been made. In a moment of profound naivety, the smiling president told the American public,

> I have got the best announcement that I think I could possibly make to America tonight ... Egypt, Britain and France have met through their Foreign Ministers and agreed to a set of principles on which to negotiate and it looks like here is a great crisis that is behind us.

Perhaps Eisenhower had one eye on election day, which was now only three and a half weeks away, but even the most charitable reading of his announcement is that it was extremely premature. He was also very, very wrong.

The Security Council voted on Saturday, 13 October. The first part of the resolution, the Six Principles, was accepted unanimously. The introduction of the follow-up was vetoed by the Soviet Union. There were two interpretations of the vote. Lloyd chose to view it as a positive precursor to further talks. Eden shared that view, at least temporarily, cabling in reply to the news that Lloyd should tell the Egyptians to ignore the veto and hold further talks in Geneva. That day, Eden addressed the Conservative Party conference. Having rather conveniently forgotten his first instincts on the night of 26 July, he painted himself as the internationalist he had been throughout his career:

> There are some who argue that we should have acted more promptly by striking back the moment Colonel Nasser seized the Canal. I do not agree. By going through every stage which the [United Nations] Charter lays down, we have given an example of restraint and respect for international undertakings.

The second interpretation was that of the French: that the UN route had now been exhausted, as the UN had failed to endorse full international administration of the canal, and that the only viable way of ending the crisis was through force. Eden would get to choose which view won the day.

The next morning, Sunday, 14 October, one French government minister and one French general flew across the Channel. On landing, they were welcomed to British soil by the French ambassador, who then had strict instructions not to accompany them to their destination.

A few hours later, Eden's quiet afternoon at the prime ministerial country house retreat of Chequers was interrupted by the arrival of two guests. After a preamble, the French official delicately inquired what the British might do if Israel attacked Egypt. Eden sarcastically replied that "he could not see himself fighting to save Nasser". The official now handed over to the French general who began to present in detail. As he spoke, Eden turned to the junior Foreign Office minister who was in room and told him, "There's no need to take notes." The French suggestion was that Israel should be encouraged to attack Egypt and to sweep across the Sinai desert towards the canal triggering a counterattack by Egyptian forces. The British and French would issue an ultimatum to end hostilities and when it was ignored would intervene "to separate the combatants". The fact that in doing so they would by default take control of the Suez Canal was merely fortuitous. As one British diplomat later noted in his diary:

> The broad idea was that there would be an Israeli attack and we should send forces to separate the contestants. There would be parachute landings and the parachutists as they fell from the sky would say *"Tiens! Voila le canal."*

The plan provided the *casus belli* Eden had been seeking since that fateful night in July.

The French were careful not to categorically state whether the Israelis were on board, but intimated that discussions had already been held, although in fact no one had yet presented the idea to the Israelis. Eden was officially non-committal, but the two Frenchman left Chequers with the decided impression that the British prime minister was already a true convert. Once the guests, whose names were erased from the visitors' book, had departed, the junior Foreign Office minister suggested that the Foreign Office's legal council should be told of the plan. Eden responded, "The lawyers are always against our doing anything. For God's sake, keep them out of it. This is a political affair."

In a moment of genius, when the Pineau did discuss the plan with Jerusalem, he presented it as an idea that came from London. Ben-Gurion noted in his diary:

> The English proposed that we should start on our own, they will protest, and when we reach the Canal they will come in as if to separate [the Israelis and Egyptians] and then they'll destroy Nasser.

After nearly three months of waiting, there was finally a tentative plan for how France and Britain might justify going to war over the canal.

# 9. SÈVRES

On 22 October a DC-4 emerged from a misty sky to touch down at an airfield outside of Paris. A small group of passengers disembarked, clustered close in the cold damp, speaking quickly and quietly in a foreign tongue. Ben-Gurion tucked his book – the Roman historian Procopius's account of the Justinian wars – under his arm and Moshe Dayan and the rest of the Israeli delegation got into black cars and drove off. A worker at the airfield spotted what he thought was the face of the Israeli prime minister beneath a broad-brimmed hat, but when he telephoned a journalist friend with his scoop, he was told he must have been mistaken.

The worker's hunch was correct: the Israelis were travelling to Sèvres for a secret meeting with the French and the British. They were planning to start a war. The setting was an appropriate one for clandestine meetings: a villa belonging to a friend of the French defence minister which had been a Resistance safe house during the Nazi occupation of France. Selwyn Lloyd arrived the same day, having travelled from Hendon on an RAF plane. Inquiries as to why he was not available in London were rebuffed by his secretary who stressed that the foreign secretary was in bed with a cold. All the planned events in his official diary had been neatly crossed out.

The French were in an extremely belligerent mood. Six days previously, French naval forces had seized a yacht off the North African coast. The *Athos* was carrying 100 tonnes of arms for Algerian rebels. It had set sail from Alexandria in Egypt. An internal French government memo recorded the arms shipment was "proof positive that Nasser was behind the [Algerian] rebellion and that he would have to go".

Sèvres was to host the secret meetings at which the plan outlined to Eden at Chequers just over a week before became policy. Pineau revelled in the subterfuge, noting that Moshe Dayan "with his black eye patch, gave the impression of a Caribbean pirate trying to board a vessel of her Britannic Majesty". Lloyd was not entirely enthusiastic for the plan – Dayan later wrote, "His whole demeanour expressed distaste, for the place the company, and the topic" – but he was still officially the man charged with captaining the British ship of state through foreign waters. He did not want it boarded by anyone and seemed disinclined to sail into hostile seas. Lloyd told the Israelis at Sèvres that it was probable that a settlement with Egypt might be reached through the UN process within seven days, but that such an outcome would only strengthen Nasser. He added, "since Her Majesty's Government considered that Nasser had to go, it was prepared to undertake military action in accordance with the latest version of the Anglo-French plan." But he did not exude an air of confidence and when he left at midnight on the first day Pineau was of the impression the British were again getting cold feet. The impression was supported by a hurried message which Lloyd dispatched immediately once he arrived back in London. It read, "I think I should make clear ... that the Government of the United Kingdom has not asked the Israeli Government to undertake an action of any kind." He insisted that he had only been "asked what would be our reactions if certain things were to happen".

In Lloyd's absence, Pineau and Dayan came up with a reasonable case for the Israelis to start the war. They would claim they were mounting an attack in the Sinai to destroy *fedayeen* bases, although there were none in the desert. Dayan added the condition that Israel should be granted a permanent annexation of at least half of the Sinai Peninsula.

The following morning, Pineau flew to London to meet with Lloyd and Eden. All through that day and into the next the Israelis debated whether to take the plunge into war. On the morning of 24 October, Ben-Gurion and Dayan took a walk together in the grounds of the villa after breakfast. They chatted over military plans, which Dayan drew on the back of a cigarette box as he had not brought any paper. Laughing, they signed it together. The British were now the final missing piece.

Pineau arrived back at Sèvres at 3 p.m. that afternoon with the good news that Eden, whom he had met after he had dinner with Lloyd, was still keen on a military operation, despite Lloyd's comments about the UN being near to a potential resolution. Lloyd's place at Sèvres was taken by Patrick Dean, a Foreign Office official and head of the Joint Intelligence Committee, while Lloyd put in a scheduled appearance in Parliament. Eden had personally briefed Dean before he left for France. He took to Sèvres the clear message that the British were unequivocally in.

Israeli representatives meet in Jerusalem to discuss the crisis, 18 October 1956. From left: Joseph Avidar (ambassador to the USSR), Jacob Tsur (ambassador to France), Abba Eban (ambassador to the US and UN representative) and Eliahu Elath with Golda Meir.

The decision made, Dayan informed the assembled company, "We will carry out such an operation that you will be able, without any doubt, to claim that there is a danger to the Canal." He added, "We won't make a declaration [of war]. We'll simply smash them." The words were music to Pineau's ears.

The parties took a break and when they returned to the room they were presented with a French-typed document to sign. It was the Sèvres Protocol. The protocol outlined that Israel would launch an attack, the British and French would call for a ceasefire and when it did not materialize they would launch military operations. The penultimate clause stated, "The arrangements of the present protocol must remain strictly secret." Pineau was insistent that everyone should sign, but Dean and his aide left the room to discuss what they should do. They had not expected anything to be written down, but neither had they been expressly instructed not to confirm anything in writing. Dean put his signature next to those of Pineau and Ben-Gurion, but stated his signing was "subject to the approval of his government". As Dean departed for London, the French and Israelis uncorked a bottle of champagne.

Ben-Gurion recorded in his diary that night:

> This is a unique opportunity, that two not so small powers will try to topple Nasser, and we shall not stand along against him while he becomes stronger ... maybe the whole situation in the Middle East will change.

Pineau and Ben-Gurion.

Dean went straight to Downing Street where he sat down with Eden, Macmillan and Rab Butler, who was leader of the House of Commons. They agreed to recommend the Sèvres plan to Cabinet the following day, but Eden was aghast when he found out that anything at all had been written down. The British copy of the protocol was burned in the Downing Street fireplace by the Cabinet secretary, while Eden ordered Dean back to Paris to "retrieve and destroy all copies". He was too late. The French simply refused, leaving Dean waiting for hours in a reception room at the Quai d'Orsay, and Ben-Gurion was already on his way back to Jerusalem with the incriminating document safely sequestered in his waistcoat pocket.

The Israelis had also left with something else from Sèvres. Just before the signing of the protocol Israel's defence minister, Shimon Peres, met alone with Mollet and an aide. In the short meeting, the French president agreed to build a heavy-water nuclear reactor at Dimona in southern Israel and supply the uranium needed to fuel it. The French parting gift, to sweeten the Sèvres deal, was to enable Israel to develop its own nuclear weapons.

On 25 October, Eden and his Cabinet convened at Downing Street. Before the meeting started, Edward Heath, the chief whip, wandered in to find the prime minister "bright-eyed and full of life". Eden told Heath, "We've got an agreement! Israel has agreed to invade Egypt. We shall then send in our own forces backed up by the French, to separate the combatants and regain the Canal." Heath afterwards claimed he tried to change Eden's mind, but that Eden simply asserted "he could not let Nasser get away with it".

Eden did not give the whole Cabinet the details of what had taken place at Sèvres. He told his colleagues that Israel was advancing preparations to attack Egypt and explained that if war broke out and the Israelis and Egyptians refused an ultimatum to halt hostilities it would provide "ample justification for Anglo-French military action against Egypt in order to safeguard the Canal". He admitted, "We must face the risk that we should be accused of collusion with Israel." There were notable objections from some of the men around the table, but Eden secured a majority in favour. Only a handful of those present knew everything, but it did not take much imagination to guess that more might be going on behind the scenes. The subsequent furious claims by some ministers that they were deceived into war were at best only half-truths.

In Washington, Dulles had no idea of the goings-on outside of Paris, but alarm bells were ringing. He told a British official, "we are quite disturbed here over the fact that there is apparently an elaborate British plan of keeping us completely in the dark as to their intentions." But Dulles and Eisenhower were preoccupied with another crisis that was a graver threat to world peace than a possible war over Suez.

# 10. "A NAIL IN MY HEAD"

The Hungarian capital sits astride the wide, slow-flowing waters of the river Danube. Budapest is a picturesque city of palaces, castles and churches and in the autumn of 1956 it was the setting for a mass uprising against Soviet rule. On the same day that Pineau flew to London to chase after Lloyd and lure Eden into the joint French-Israeli war plan for Suez, more than 200,000 protestors gathered outside the national parliament in Budapest. They chanted patriotic songs and as the protest carried on into the night, one group tore to the ground a thirty-foot statue of Joseph Stalin.

Since the end of Second World War, Hungary had been behind the Iron Curtain. It was one of the nations whose fate was initially cynically decided by Churchill and Stalin in Moscow in October 1944, when Churchill wrote down a list of Balkan countries and alongside noted 'percentages' of influence for the Soviets and the Western allies. Hungary had supposedly been fifty-fifty, but by early 1945 Soviet forces had simply taken complete control. Stalin installed a Communist leadership, which was changed by order of Moscow

While the Politburo deliberated, the statue of Stalin was torn down.

in 1953. Imre Nagy, a Hungarian former KGB informant, transpired to be somewhat of a reformer, albeit a cautious one. He released a number of key Hungarian politicians and thinkers who had been imprisoned under his predecessor and did just enough to find himself summoned to Moscow in 1955 where he was promptly fired.

His replacement found himself officially leading a country which was far less accepting of a Soviet puppet. Individual moments of opposition to authority converged: Soviet troops were shouted at in the streets, there were demands for the head of the Hungarian Catholic Church to be released from imprisonment and in October a group of students, professors and even a few politicians occupied a printers and churned out leaflets demanding the withdrawal of Soviet troops, free elections and the creation of a new caretaker government under Imre Nagy, who had been permitted to live quietly in Hungary since his removal from power. The leaflets were distributed all over Budapest. On 23 October, the Ministry of the Interior banned all protests, to no avail, as thousands congregated in the capital. Khrushchev received an urgent message from his puppet leader: "You must come to Moscow urgently for talks." Khrushchev was disinclined to talk, especially when he received direct reports of what was taking place in the Hungarian capital; the Soviet ambassador reported to Moscow that troops were needed on the streets.

Hungarian leader Imre Nagy.

As the demonstrations continued in the darkness, the Politburo convened in Moscow. Vyacheslav Molotov – the chairman of the Council Ministers and former Soviet foreign secretary who had met and got on well with Eden on multiple occasions – told the assembled company, "Hungary is coming apart." Khrushchev saw Hungary not as an isolated case of a disgruntled populace, but as the thin end of the wedge. "If we leave Hungary that would encourage the American, British and French imperialists. They would understand this as our weakness and would be on the offensive." The generals were in agreement and Khrushchev was clear: "There's no alternative but to send soldiers without delay." While the Politburo had been in session, Stalin's statue in Budapest had been hauled to the ground. By the time the meeting ended, Hungarian students were joyously standing on the head of the former leader of the Soviet Union.

Molotov (third from left) knew Eden and Churchill from their meetings during the war.

The Politburo contrived to stage-manage the situation. In an apparent concession it was announced that Nagy had been reinstated as Hungarian leader, although it was not a role he wanted, and shortly afterwards the first announcement was followed by a second. It was claimed that Nagy had made an appeal to the Soviet Union to come and restore order; in fact he had done no such thing, although Moscow later exhibited a document in his name. In the early hours of 24 October, 6,000 Soviet soldiers with accompanying tanks headed toward the Hungarian capital. Khrushchev could not sleep that night. He later recalled that his worry over Budapest "was like a nail in my head".

By midday on 24 October there was fighting on the streets. Soviet tanks and soldiers had opened fire on civilians and the violence had escalated; demonstrators began production lines of Molotov cocktails. Protests were also underway in other Hungarian cities.

When news of the scale of what was going on reached Washington, Dulles remarked to a colleague over the phone he was "worried that it will be said that here are the great moments and when they came these fellows were ready to stand up and die, we were caught napping and doing nothing".

On 25 October, Soviet-controlled radio was broadcasting across Budapest that Soviet troops had "liquidated the counter-revolutionary putsch attempt" the day before.

Napoleon in Egypt. He was ordered to "arrange for the cutting of the Isthmus of Suez" but died before the Suez Canal was constructed.

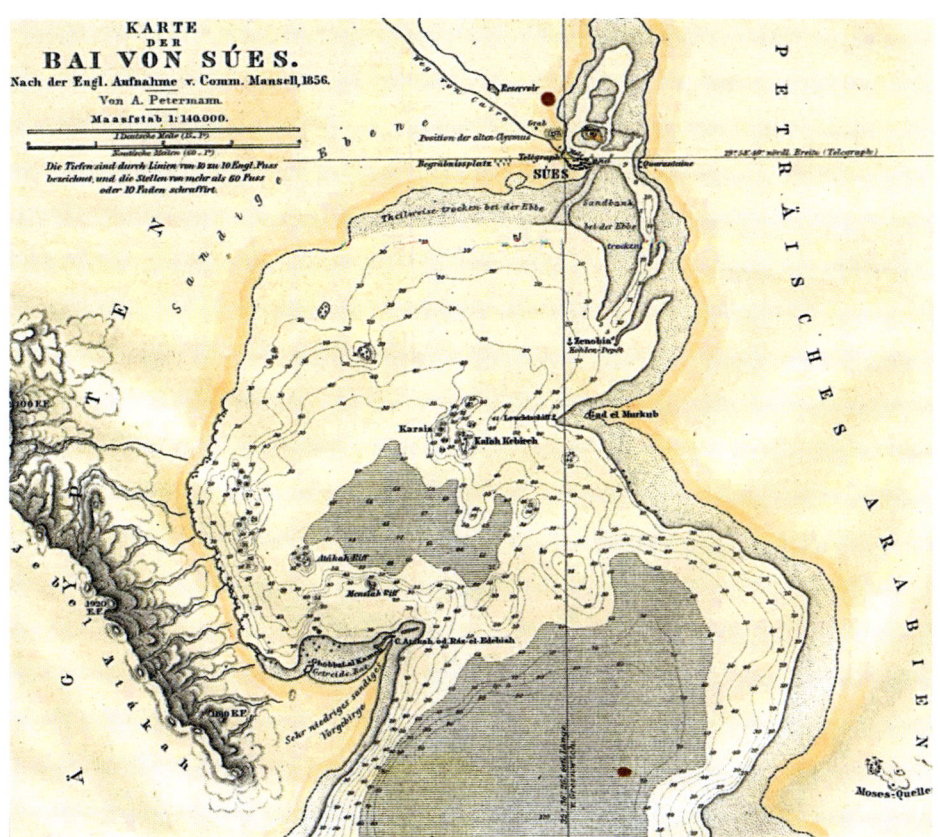

Suez Bay, Egypt. Justus Perthes's Geographische Anstalt, 1856.

*Left*: A caricature of Le Vicomte de Lesseps, the original caption reading: "He suppressed an isthmus." *Vanity Fair*, 27 November 1869.

*Below*: The house of Ferdinand de Lesseps, promoter of the Suez Canal, in Ismailia, Egypt.

Thirteen years after the opening of the canal, Britain went to war in Egypt to safeguard shipping and put down the nationalist Urabi revolt.

Port Said, the Arab Quarter, 1890.

Port Said, the port, 1890.

The Royal Navy battleship HMS *Howe*, flagship of the Commander-in-Chief Pacific Fleet, Admiral Sir Bruce Fraser, passing through the Suez Canal on its way to the Pacific, 14 July 1944, only twelve years before the Crisis.

*Above*: Al-Ahram front page, 29 July 1956.

*Left*: The British prime minister's country retreat of Chequers.

The RAF's Canberra was a state-of-the-art bomber.

De Havilland Sea Venom FAW22 (DH-112) seen in the markings of 809 Naval Air Squadron during the Suez Crisis of 1956.

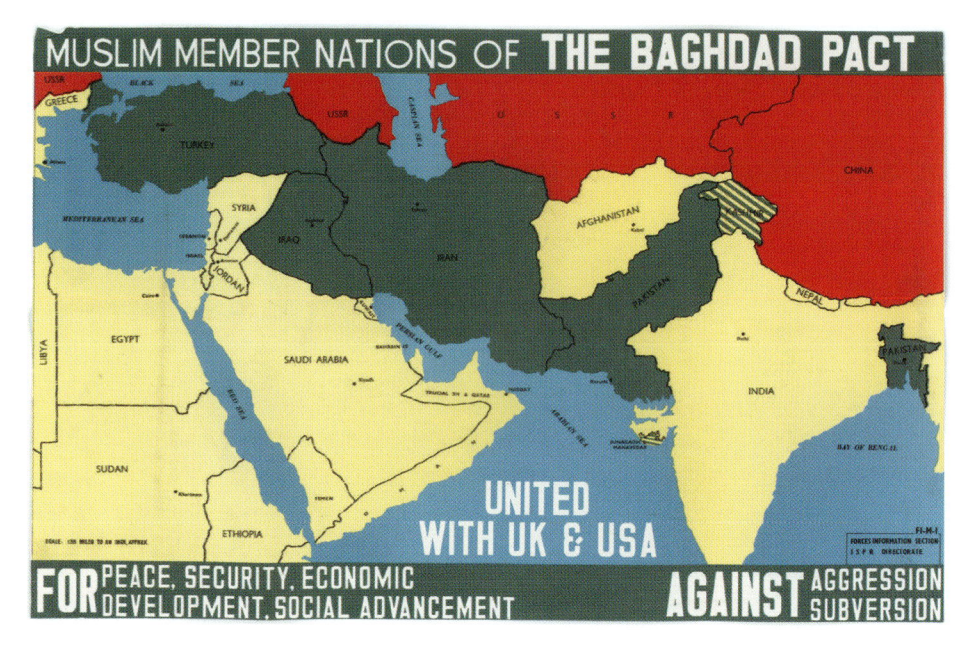

A Pakistan-produced propaganda poster espousing the virtues of membership of the Baghdad Pact.

Carrier, Personnel Half-Track M3, generally known as the 'White Half-Track', which was used by Allied forces worldwide throughout World War II, the Korean War, Suez, Vietnam and even later. This is a Soviet example on display at the Patriot Museum Complex, Moscow.

*Left*: A Soviet propaganda postcard from 1958. The British lion has lost its tail and the French cockerel its feathers. The text reads, "The Anglo-French military intervention in Egypt ended up as a total fiasco. As a result, prestige and political position of the UK and France were weakened, economic difficulties intensified."

*Below*: The Suez Canal near the town of Kantara.

Ian Fleming's villa in Jamaica which he lent to Eden in November 1956.

*Right*: Harold Macmillan pictured with John F. Kennedy five years after the Suez Crisis.

*Below*: The U.S. circumvented the power of the British and French vetoes in the UN Security Council by securing a resolution against the Suez action in the General Assembly.

United States war planes over Kuwait during the 1991 Gulf War.

U.S. tanks in Baghdad, November 2003.

The amphibious assault ship USS *Kearsarge* transits the Suez Canal on 22 April 2005, behind the guided-missile destroyer USS *Gonzalez*.

*Above*: Port Said, Suez Canal Authority, as seen in 2007.

*Left*: Egyptian military guard post at the brink of the Suez Canal, February 2008.

Soviet armour in the Hungarian capital, Budapest.

But there were still protestors braving the streets. A crowd, which may have included as many as 20,000, gathered in a Budapest central square opposite the nation's parliament and faced off against a line of Soviet tanks. What followed is disputed, but what is clear is that the protestors found themselves under sustained fire for around fifteen minutes. Hundreds were killed, although the official Soviet-recorded figure later put the dead at twenty-two. A dispatch sent by a *New York Times* reporter holed up in the U.S. embassy noted the square "was strewn with dead and dying Hungarian men and women shot down by Russian tanks ... the tanks fired not only their machine guns but their big guns. The insurgents were unarmed." An observer from the British embassy saw twelve trucks later arrive to take away bodies. When Eden's Cabinet met on 25 October, there was remarkably no discussion of Hungary. It was not even on the agenda.

At 9 a.m. Washington time on 26 October, as Israeli forces stepped up their mobilization, Eisenhower and Dulles were in a National Security Council meeting. Hungary was the first thing talked about. Dulles announced that the events in Hungary were the most serious threat yet to Soviet control of their "satellites". Eisenhower was wary and he wanted to know if it was suggested the U.S. was involved – as was already being rumoured in Moscow: "might they not be tempted to resort to very extreme measures and even to precipitate a global war?"

When Dulles and Eisenhower spoke again on the phone that evening it was clear both were oscillating between joy at the sight of Soviet-controlled nation trying to wrench itself free and concern that its freedom might be extremely short lived. Dulles proposed taking the situation to the UN Security Council. When he put the phone down he dictated a message for Lloyd in London, asking for British support, noting "The revolt is assuming proportions which may in turn bring Red [Soviet] counteraction of major proportions."

Dulles himself gave a speech the following evening in which his focus was on the crisis in Europe. He declared "The weakness of Soviet imperialism is being made manifest" and went on to assert America's support for liberty everywhere. However, in a clear message to Moscow agreed with Eisenhower beforehand, he insisted the U.S. had "no ulterior purpose in desiring the independence [of Hungary]".

On the streets of Budapest, sporadic fighting was still taking place and even some Soviet soldiers had defected to join what was now a ragtag group of rebels. Imre Nagy, reinstated and framed as the man who had called in the tanks by Moscow, struggled with disparate elements of his own government, including Communist figures who wanted to force the Hungarian army to clear the streets and liberals who proposed he should become the hero of the revolution the chanting students had imagined him to be five days before.

For almost everyone except the British and the French, the crisis in Hungary was more pressing than Suez, which appeared to be headed for some sort of drawn-out negotiated settlement, to the embarrassment of Britain and France. At the Politburo meeting on 28 October, Khrushchev remarked, "The English and the French are in a real mess in Egypt. We shouldn't get caught in the same company. But we must not foster illusions. We are saving face."

# 11. THE JORDANIAN COMPLICATION

More than one Middle Eastern country faced the threat of potential invasion in the autumn of 1956. War between Egypt and Israel was deemed an inevitability in Jerusalem, but the Israeli desire for lasting border security also drew Dayan's and Ben-Gurion's attention east, to Jordan.

The country of Jordan had been established by the British after the First World War and given to the second son of the Sharif of Mecca as a thank-you for wartime Arab support against the Turks. The Hashemite dynasty hailed from Arabia, a fact that forever made their position as rulers a precarious one. When Jordan became fully independent after the Second World War, King Abdullah renewed a treaty with Britain in which Britain granted military and monetary assistance to his rule. The Jordanian Army was even officially under the command of a British general, John Bagot Glubb, an enigmatic, silver-moustached Lancashire Englishman.

But the close connection was an uneasy one. In March 1956, after refusing the British advances to the join the Baghdad Pact, the king had dismissed Glubb, along with other

The Jordanian Army was led by the British commander John Bagot Glubb.

British advisers, in a show of force to prove to rankling public opinion that the Hashemite monarch was, in fact, master of his nation's fate. The action shocked Eden, who initially told colleagues he was "utterly mystified by the whole event", even suggesting that the young Jordanian king "has brainstorms like his father" – a reference to Hussein's father's troubles with schizophrenia, which had led to his abdication and confinement in a sanitorium. Eden faced strong criticism in the House of Commons from the Opposition for what appeared to be the unravelling of old alliances in the Middle East and got into petty arguments with members who interrupted his closing speech. *The New York Times* even reported he was "subjected to a storm of vituperation and abuse beyond anything heard in the Commons since the last days of Neville Chamberlain's prime ministership". Eden was angered by the response and utterly convinced that the actions of the young monarch were not down to Jordanian public opinion – even though there had been protests on the streets of Amman – but were in fact Nasser's fault. The Egyptian leader was encouraging Arab nationalism across the region and Cairo radio was as damning of British involvement in Jordan as in Egypt. Eden was outraged shortly afterwards to learn that the Foreign Office were in discussions with U.S. representatives to see if they could undermine Nasser's position. He telephoned a senior Foreign Office official who was having lunch at the Savoy and yelled down the open line, "What's all this nonsense about isolating Nasser or 'neutralizing' him, as you call it? I want him murdered, and if you and the Foreign Office don't agree, then you'd better come to the Cabinet and explain why!" Eden finished the tirade with the assertion he didn't "give a damn if there's anarchy and chaos in Egypt" before hanging up. The prime minister calmed down after his outburst, but it demonstrated that there was one man, above all, whom he considered responsible for Britain's problems overseas.

Jordan also had a complicated relationship with neighbouring Israel. Glubb had led Jordanian forces to take control of the West Bank during the 1948 Israeli war of independence and although the action was officially occupying the regions granted to the Arabs under the UN partition plan, British-led Jordanian troops ended up fighting Israelis. Three years later, the first king of Jordan was assassinated by a Palestinian after rumours circulated that he was planning to make a permanent peace deal with Israel.

In 1956, the 21-year-old King Hussein had no intention of being on the receiving end of the same fate as one of his predecessors, but at the same time he was not angling for a war. Like Egypt, Jordan had also become a base for Palestinian *fedayeen* guerrillas who targeted Israel and on 10 September 1956 the Israelis struck back. Paratroops occupied and demolished a police station and several military positions across the Jordanian border, in the process killing thirty-nine Jordanians. Violence flared up again a few weeks later, so that by the time the UN Security Council was debating the Suez Crisis, it was not impossible that Israel and Jordan might go to war.

The great complication was that, because of the Anglo-Jordanian Treaty, if Israel attacked Jordan, Britain was duty bound to come to her aid, a fact the Foreign Office had formally reminded the Israelis of after the action in September. The military staff even drew up a plan for a British action against Israel, named Operation *Cordage*, in which British bombers would attack Israeli air bases alongside a naval blockade and military assistance to Jordan intended to halt any escalating conflict in its tracks. Helpfully for the British government, to an outside observer it was hard to tell whether the mobilization of British air and naval forces in the autumn of 1956 would be deployed against Egypt or Israel. The dual plans of *Musketeer* and *Cordage* aided secrecy and kept U.S. officials guessing.

They were not the only ones. As late as 20 October, British commanders in the Mediterranean were still under the impression that they were moving their ships to a seventy-two-hour readiness status in preparation for either an attack on Egypt, or on Israel. One

As a result of the Anglo-Jordanian Treaty, Jordan's young king, Hussein, could rely on British support if Israel attacked.

message between Mediterranean commanders even contemplated that both operations might be mounted one after the other, noting, "If Musketeer is likely to be ordered closely after Cordage, it will be necessary to withdraw the carrier effort from Cordage once the Israeli air force has been neutralized."

For the soldiers themselves there was equal confusion. When 21 year old Second Lieutenant Peter Mayo of 42 Commando embarked on HMS *Simla* at Malta, no one knew where they were headed. He recorded in his diary, "Were we going to Jordan, Hong Kong, Singapore, or to be sent through the canal with a convoy just to see what happened? The whole thing seems pretty shambolic to me."

The Israelis also joined in the deception. All reserves were called up in mid-October, but the deployment of ready units was varied enough to make it possible that they might be attacking either Egypt or Jordan. When the U.S. ambassador dined with Lloyd in London on the evening of 28 October, he asked the foreign secretary if he knew why the Israelis had mobilized. Lloyd deliberately misled the ambassador. "Britain had warned the Israelis," he said, "using very strong language indeed, that, if they attacked Jordan, they would have Britain to reckon with."

## Suez Crisis 1956

Nasser receiving the Indian military delegation at the presidency, February 1956.

Jordanian Army Chief of Staff Radi Annab standing next to Nasser during Friday prayers in the last week of Ramadan, 4 May 1956.

## The Jordanian Complication

King Hussein of Jordan (left), President Nasser of Egypt and his Chief of Staff Abdel Hakim Amer before signing the Egyptian–Jordanian–Iraqi defence pact in Cairo, May 1967.

When the US sought British assistance in Vietnam, Prime Minister Harold Wilson replied, "Most members of Parliament think Washington is morally in the wrong. And many remember the American reaction to Suez."

# 12. STORMS IN THE DESERT

The Americans were getting jumpy. Just as dawn broke over the city on 29 October, a diplomatic car arrived unannounced at the Israeli Ministry of Defence in Tel Aviv. Inside the vehicle was an anxious counsellor from the U.S. embassy, who delivered a message to Ben-Gurion from the president in which he stated, "I feel compelled to emphasize the dangers inherent in the present situation and to urge your Government to do nothing which would endanger the peace." It was a credit to the smoke and mirrors exercise being conducted that the Americans still thought Israel might invade Jordan.

The British ambassador, who had no idea of what had taken place at Sèvres, pitched up to see Golda Meir who calmly informed him that no hostilities were intended against Jordan and that the mass call-up of army reservists was simply so Israel could be "prepared".

At 2 p.m. that afternoon, four Israeli aircraft flew twelve feet above the desert across the Sinai to cut through telegraph wires as the first of Dayan's mechanized columns crossed into Egyptian territory. The war had begun.

Israeli armoured column advancing from Abu-Ageila, 3 November 1956.

*Storms in the Desert*

Nasser was at home in Cairo for his second son's birthday. Just after 5-year-old Abdul had blown out the candles on his cake, the Egyptian leader was quietly informed of the news and he slipped out of the room, telling his wife he had been called to a meeting. The news, such as it was, was perplexing. It was unclear if the Israeli troops spotted in the desert were part of small incursion or something larger, but Egyptian forces were ordered to cross the canal in readiness to respond. The editor of Egypt's *Al-Ahram* newspaper received a call from his friend the president that evening. Nasser said, "Something very strange is happening. The Israelis are in the Sinai and they seem to be fighting the sands ... it looks to us as if all they want to do is start up sand storms in the desert."

Shortly before Nasser put through his call to the editor of *Al-Ahram*, sixteen Israeli Douglas DC-3s flew into the Negev carrying 395 paratroopers who were dropped over Mitla Pass, thirty miles east of Suez.

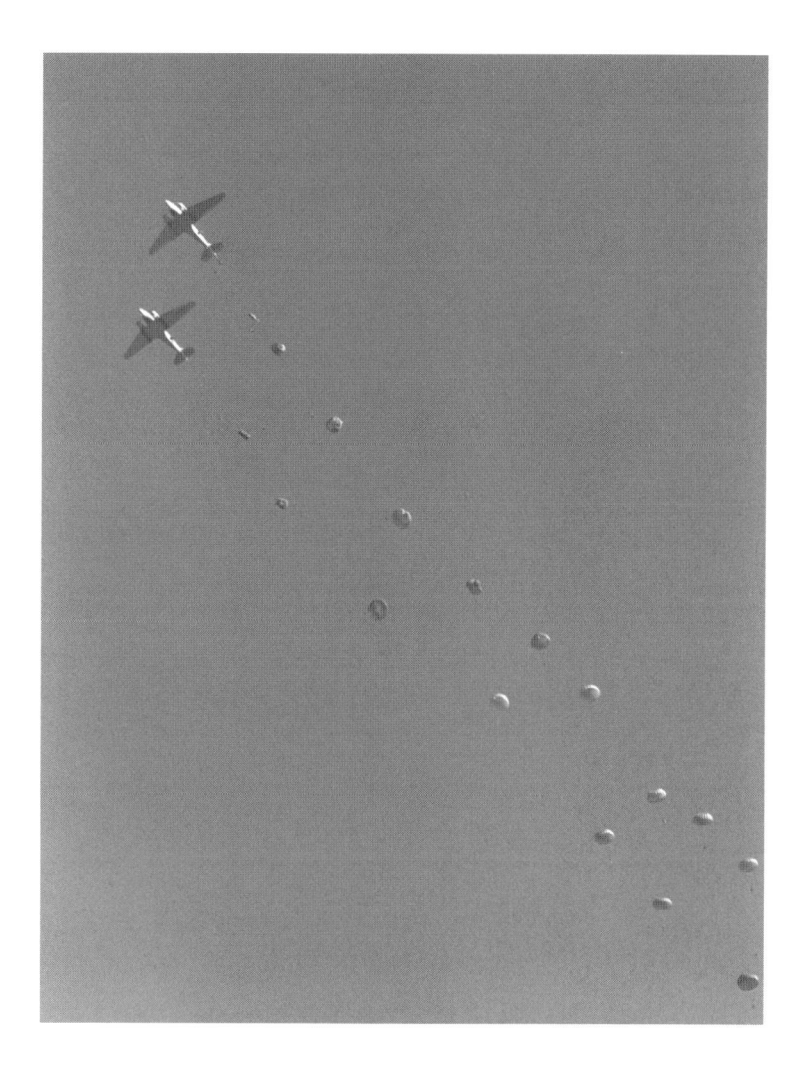

Israeli paratroops jumping from a DC-3 aircraft.

Their progress was being watched from high above by RAF aerial reconnaissance aircraft. In London, Eden was on the phone every fifteen minutes to the chief of air staff demanding to know if there was any news from the Egyptian–Israeli frontier. Finally, later than expected, he heard that trails of parachutists' canopies had been spotted, dotting the desert behind transport aircraft. The Sèvres plan could now unfold.

Eisenhower found out about the Israeli attack when he returned to the White House at 7 p.m. Washington time after a campaign trip to Florida. He exploded at Dulles:

> Foster, you tell 'em, Goddamnit, that we're going to apply sanctions, we're going to the United Nations, we're going to do everything that there is to so we can stop this thing ... nothing justifies double crossing us.

But there were more shocks to come.

The next morning, Lloyd spoke to officials at the State Department and insisted that Britain had not yet decided how to respond. A few hours later Eisenhower began drafting a message to Eden. It was long and friendly enough but admitted there was "a very sad state of confusion" between "your Government and ours". Eisenhower was politely demanding to know what the hell was going on.

Mitla Pass in the Sinai Desert.

The president's cable reached London at 4.30 p.m., just as Eden got to his feet in the House of Commons. He began by outlining to the House the increasing "tension on the frontiers of Israel", citing incursions by guerrilla fighters and Egypt's growing military strength, moving on to inform Parliament of the progress of the Israeli advance which was now "in the neighbourhood of the Canal". He calmly stated, "I must tell the House that very grave issues are at stake, and that unless hostilities can very quickly be stopped free passage through the Canal will be jeopardized." Britain and France, he said, were doing everything possible to involve the UN Security Council, but added, "in order to separate the belligerents and to guarantee freedom of transit through the Canal by the ships of all nations we have asked the Egyptian Government to agree that Anglo-French forces should move temporarily – I repeat, temporarily – into key positions at Port Said, Ismailia and Suez." Finally, he concluded that if Israel and Egypt did not halt hostilities within twelve hours, "British and French forces will intervene in whatever strength may be necessary to secure compliance."

Eden's statement in Parliament was perfectly timed to ensure that no progress could be made on any recourse to the Security Council so there was no stopping the British and French ultimatum. The debate went on in Parliament late into the night, but Eden won an Opposition-tabled vote of no-confidence by 270 votes to 218. It was close, but Eden had carried the day.

The ultimatum caused considerable disquiet. Eden's former principal private secretary, who had moved to a position in the Foreign Office by 1956, noted in his diary that night:

> It seems to have *every* fault. It is clearly not genuinely impartial, since the Israelis are nowhere near the Canal ... the Americans were not consulted; the UN is flouted; we are about to be at war without the nation or Parliament having been given a hint of it. We think A[thony].E[den]. has gone off his head.

Eisenhower's response, when news of Eden's ultimatum reached Washington, was entirely unprintable; one journalist later reported that the White House "crackled with barracks room language". Eisenhower put through a call to Downing Street and, mistaking one of Eden's aides for the British prime minister, launched into a tirade of "unshirted hell". By the time Eden got to the phone the president had hung up.

Israel's representative at the UN, Abba Eban, spoke at an emergency meeting of the UN Security Council in New York later that day. He asserted Israel was taking action against Egypt "to eliminate the bases from which armed Egyptian units, under the special care and authority of Colonel Nasser, invade Israel's territory for murder, [and] sabotage." Highlighting the fact that Israeli ships were barred from the canal, he added, "The State of Israel has had to distort the entire pattern of its economy, to bear illicit burdens running into tens of millions of pounds, in order to compensate for the impact of this piratical system which Egypt has established on a great artery of the world's communications."

The Americans were not impressed. With the blessing of the White House, the U.S. representative tabled a resolution calling for the complete withdrawal of Israeli forces and the suspension of all military, economic and financial aid to Israel until they did so, plus a commitment that all Security Council members would refrain from the use or threat of force in the area. Just after 11.30 p.m. New York time, the Council voted. The only two members who voted against the resolution were Britain and France. It was the first time Britain had used her veto.

During the night of 30 October, air crew in Cyprus worked through the darkness to ready their Canberras and paint yellow and black recognition stripes on the wings of each aircraft. The first targets were to be the Egyptian airfields which were home to the Russian-made Ilyushin jet bombers that Ben-Gurion was so concerned would sortie against Israeli cities.

Abba Eban's career included positions as an ambassador and Israel's foreign minister. He was a true diplomat who always saw war as a last resort; he described Sèvres as a "grotesquely eccentric" plan.

The day before, the Royal Navy aircraft carriers *Eagle*, *Bulwark* and *Albion* had sailed from Malta. They joined up with two French carriers and two light carriers transporting Royal Marine commandos and twenty-four assault helicopters. The slower-moving amphibious force followed behind but would take six days to reach Port Said. As the deadline for the ultimatum passed, French Mystère fighter-bombers previously transferred to Israeli airfields prepared to support the Israeli Air Force's French-made aircraft in attacks on Egyptian forces in the Sinai, and at 4.14 p.m. GMT on 31 October the Canberras went into action.

At the last minute, their target was changed. News reached London that American nationals were evacuating from Cairo and at that very moment travelling on a road alongside the airfield the Canberras were targeting. Eden directly ordered them to change target to a different military airfield. The pilots had only ten minutes' warning before taking off and their navigators had to re-route their flight plans in the air. The desperate alteration minutes before take-off led to an error. Under the stress of changing target and scanning the skies for MiG-15 interceptors potentially flown by Russian pilots,

The front page of the Egyptian newspaper *Al-Ahram*, 30 October 1956. The main headline reads "Israel attacks Egypt".

several Canberras missed the military airfield and ended up instead bombing Cairo International Airport. Nasser was standing on a roof watching the planes over the blacked-out capital and as soon as he realized they were jet bombers, which the Israeli Air Force did not possess, he knew the initial assessment that it was simply an attack by Israel was gravely wrong.

The RAF post-operation report noted the bombing of Cairo International instead of the intended target was "unfortunate" but added, "the last-minute change of plan ... made an error highly probable." The Anglo-French operation had started later than Ben-Gurion had been led to believe it would, twelve hours after the ultimatum officially ended. The Israeli prime minister had angrily cabled the French at midday:

> At this hour we are still without news of an Anglo-French operation against the Egyptian airfields. We have parachuted battalions close to the Canal with the sole aim of serving your purposes ... According to the Protocol, your operation should have started this morning ... The members of the Government are asking me if we have been abandoned.

Just over four hours later, RAF aircraft were in the air over Egypt.

An American U-2 reconnaissance plane flying out of Adana in Turkey passed over Cairo airport at high altitude just as the first waves of British bombers were attacking. Twenty minutes later the spy plane returned for a routine second flypast and photographed rows of burning aircraft. The intelligence confirmed Eisenhower's suspicions that the entire Suez military operation had been a pre-arranged scheme.

Inchas airfield following an attack by Fleet Air Arm Sea Hawks.

"Bombs, by God," Eisenhower yelled, "What does Anthony think he's doing?" His marginally calmer, slightly later assessment was astute: "I've just never seen a great power make such a mess and botch of things," the livid President told his aides. "Of course, there's nobody, in a war, I'd rather have fighting alongside me than the British. But this thing! My God."

Dulles was emotional, telling an aide they were entering "the gravest hours of Anglo-French-American relations … for three weeks I have had suspicions about what has just happened today." He then went on to compare the British and French action to "the methods of Soviet totalitarianism in Hungary." Dulles articulated the reality of what was to come, admitting to the CIA director, "there would be a strain on the Br[itish] and Fr[ench] and it will be economic and [come] quickly."

Eisenhower was keen to disavow all knowledge of what increasingly looked like a conspiracy. At 7 p.m. on 31 October, the president addressed the nation. The text had been through multiple drafts and while the writers were squirrelled away, the president had gone outside to hit golf balls. By the time he sat down in front of the cameras he was, as *The New York Times* observed, "grave". He told the American public, "The United States was not consulted in any way about any phase of these actions. Nor were we informed of them in advance." He asserted that the U.S.

> will not condone armed aggression no matter who the attacker … We cannot, in the world, any more than in our own nation subscribe to one law for the weak, another for the strong; one law for those opposing us, another for those allied with us.

Britain and France were officially on their own. That evening, the usually alcoholically restrained Eisenhower downed two Scotches before dinner and three afterwards. As the bombs rained down on Egypt, Nasser ordered a 320-foot freighter be sunk in the waterway. For the first time since the crisis began, the Suez Canal was blocked.

A downed Egyptian MiG-15.

## Suez Crisis 1956

حاربوا من قريه الى قريه ومن مكان الى مكان

During the crisis, the cartoonist Ronald Searle (the creator of St. Trinian's School) was commissioned to do the artwork for a set of leaflets that was to be dropped over Egypt in support of the invasion by British and French troops. This leaflet shows Nasser in a none-too-glowing light.

Egyptian troop deployment.

*Storms in the Desert*

An Israeli officer at Mitla Pass.

Moshe Dayan addressing the IDF's 9th Brigade at Sharm el-Sheikh.

# 13. FROM RUSSIA, WITH LOVE

In Moscow, the response to the flagrant aggression against Egypt was not what Nasser had hoped for. The focus on Hungary meant that the frantic calls for help from Cairo – Nasser messaged Khrushchev, "We desperately need air support for our troops" – went unanswered. Khrushchev told the Egyptian ambassador at a diplomatic reception in the Russian capital, "We are full of admiration for the way in which you are resisting aggression . . . but unfortunately there is no way in which we can help you militarily. But we are going to mobilize world public opinion."

The real Soviet response to the invasion did not take place until a week later, when four letters were dispatched from Russia to Eden, Mollet, Ben-Gurion and Eisenhower. The letters were signed by Bulganin as Soviet premier, but the wording had been approved by Khrushchev. In the letter to Ben-Gurion, the Soviets accused Israel of "acting as an instrument of foreign imperialist forces" – not unusual rhetoric, but language which for once was actually true – adding darkly, "this cannot fail to have an effect on the future of Israel and jeopardize its very existence as a state ... We hope that the government of Israel will understand and properly appraise this warning."

Eden replied to the letter addressed to him with the riposte that Soviet forces were crushing an independence movement in Hungary: "At such a time it ill becomes the Soviet Government to speak of the actions of Her Majesty's Government as barbaric."

To Mollet, Bulganin openly threatened nuclear war:

> What kind of position would France be in if she were subjected to an attack by other states possessing terrible modern devices of destruction? ... We hope that at this critical moment the French government will show soberness in its assessment of the situation that has arisen and will draw the appropriate conclusions.

However, the threat was rather tempered by the message to Eisenhower which instead proposed a collaboration:

> On us lies special responsibility to put [a] stop to war, and to restore peace and tranquillity to [the] area of [the] Near and Middle East ... If this war is not stopped, it is fraught with danger and can grow into [a] third world war.

Bulganin's letter proposed joint U.S.–Soviet intervention to stop the armed conflict. Molotov appeared to take the proposal rather too literally, telling Khrushchev that Eisenhower would never agree to it, to which the Soviet leader responded, "Of course he won't, but by putting him in the position of having to refuse, we'll expose the hypocrisy of his public statement condemning the attack against Egypt."

In fact, a day before the letters were dispatched, the Politburo had decided it had no intention of really going to war over Suez. As the Soviet foreign minister later admitted, "There was a firm decision not to bring the matter to the point of an armed conflict."

The Russians were still entirely occupied with Hungary. On 30 October, two Politburo representatives arrived in Budapest in an apparently conciliatory mood. They agreed to pull back Soviet troops and to negotiate Hungary's withdrawal from the Warsaw Pact (the Soviet equivalent of NATO) and the tanks rolled out of the capital. Two days later Nagy received reports that the withdrawal had been short lived and that more soldiers had crossed the border; in total there were 200,000 soldiers and 4,000 tanks. On hearing the news of the impending arrival of more Soviet troops, he made a bold move. He telephoned Moscow and formally and unilaterally pulled Hungary out of the Warsaw Pact. Officially, Hungary was now neutral. That afternoon, he took to the airwaves. "We appeal to our neighbours, countries near and far, to respect the unalterable decision of our people." In the face of the oncoming onslaught he encouraged the population, "Protect and strengthen with revolutionary determination ... our country, the free, independent, democratic and neutral Hungary." Sadly, none of the neighbours or countries near and far who were listening were planning on doing anything to help.

Angry letters and promises to mobilize world public opinion were of little assistance to Egyptian armed forces who faced serious losses even while the arrival of British and French amphibious forces was still several days away. The bombing of Egyptian air bases was supremely ineffective – the only one put out of action was deliberately rendered unusable by the Egyptians themselves – but, nevertheless, more than 200 Egyptian aircraft were destroyed on the ground. The feared Ilyushin-28 bombers were taken out not by the Canberras but by American-built but French-owned F-84 Thunderjet fighter-bombers which found and destroyed them at the air base in Luxor where they had relocated.

Command and control in the air was laughably poor at times, with one RAF air marshal admitting afterwards, "if we had been up against an enemy with even a

Soviet Il-28 bombers.

The credit for neutralizing the threat of the Russian Il-28 bombers went to French pilots flying American-made F-84 Thunderjets.

modicum of fighting qualities with the modern aircraft and equipment the Egyptians had, the situation would have been different." The Israeli urgency to attack before Egyptian aircrew were properly trained on their newly purchased Soviet hardware proved a sensible precaution.

The French were not even trying to maintain the pretence of going to war to make peace by separating the combatants and were providing close air support to Israeli ground troops in the Sinai; a number of French aircraft were even painted with the Star of David. When Eden found out he messaged Mollet, "Actions of this sort, which cannot possibly remain secret, are extremely embarrassing ... Nothing could do more harm to our role as peacemakers than to be identified in this way with one of the parties."

Eden didn't know and would have been even more upset to learn that French planes based in Cyprus had airdropped vehicles and supplies to the Israeli paratroops on the night they landed in the Mitla Pass, even before Eden had announced the joint ultimatum. The incident demonstrates the difference of perspective of Eden's and Mollet's administrations: Eden genuinely seemed to believe that the Sèvres secret would not out and the world would be taken in by the ultimatum, but the French were far less concerned now that they had finally been allowed to get their war underway.

Israeli paratroops in the Mitla Pass pause in their foxholes to clean their weapons, 10 October 1956.

A moral victory was also secured when eighteen Canberras bombed Cairo Radio off air. The British immediately replaced Nasser's propaganda with their own, broadcasting 'Voice of Britain' on the same frequency. Memorable messages included a Biblical-style prophecy of woe: "O Egyptian people ... Why has this befallen you? ... because Abdul Nasser went mad and seized the Suez Canal which is of vital importance to the world."

On the ground, Dayan's forces found that many Egyptians fought harder than expected. In an effort to gain every advantage possible, the Israelis were taking into action the latest hardware they had received from the French, including AMX light tanks. Ariel Sharon, the commander of 202 Brigade who would go on to be a future Israeli prime minister, recorded, "We had pressed them into use despite the fact they had arrived without any tools. There was no way to even change a tyre." His forces had linked up with the paratroops dropped on Mitla Pass on the second day of the offensive, vehicles mostly intact.

The desert coastline stronghold of Al-Arish was helpfully softened up by heavy fire from the six-inch guns of the French Second World War cruiser *Georges Leygues*. However, the Israeli advance was slow as they faced stiff opposition until the early hours of 1 November, when Nasser ordered his generals to evacuate the whole of the Sinai and take up defensive positions near the canal.

The amphibious force was still "swimming" its measured way from Malta, travelling – as dictated by convoy tradition – at the pace of the slowest vessel, which was a paltry

## Suez Crisis 1956

Israeli AMX tanks.

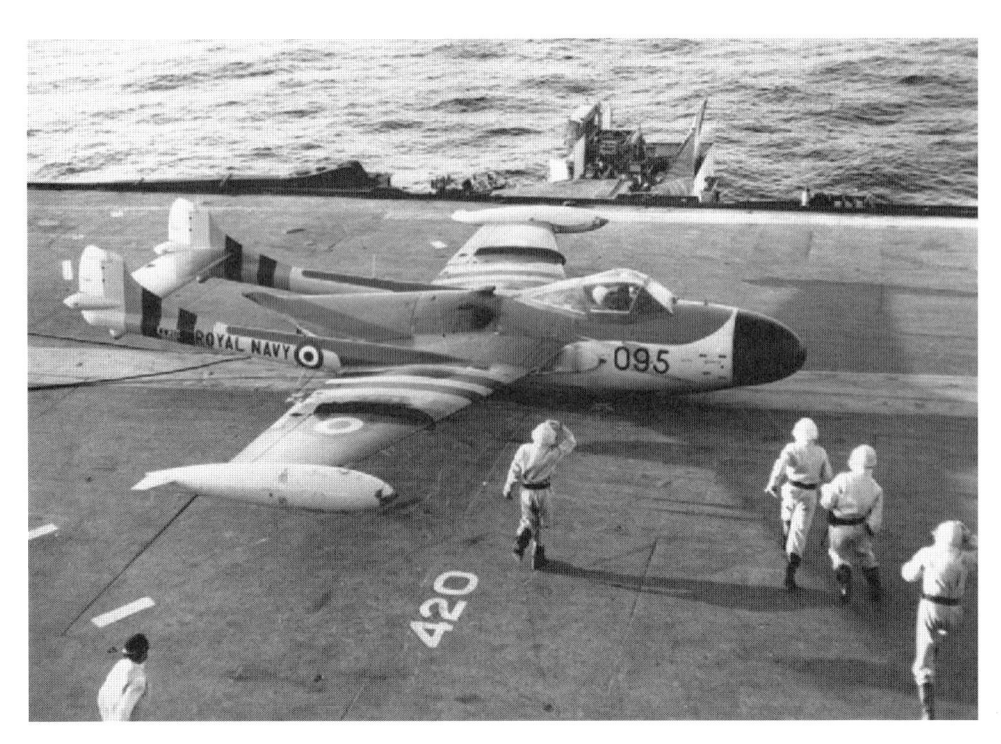

The air attacks from Cyprus were supported by Fleet Air Arm Sea Venom sorties from carriers off the Egyptian coast.

10 knots. Their progress was not exactly secret. On 30 October, *The New York Times* reported "the largest naval concentration seen in the Mediterranean since World War II."

Pineau and the French sought to speed things up. An internal military message noted:

> Information received from Israel gives the impression that the Egyptian army is beaten and routed. Even if there is some exaggeration this success must certainly be exploited ... Consider especially a light operation, mounted very rapidly!

At a meeting in London it was even suggested that rather than going to the bother of asking the paratroops to jump out of aeroplanes, a French battleship could just steam into Port Said harbour with 1,000 of them on board. The gloriously colonial-style military solution was discounted when it was pointed out that the Egyptians had in all probability already mined the harbour approach. With the prospect of action against Britain and France at the UN looming, French commanders pushed for paratroops to be dropped no later than 3 November. But if they dropped along the canal they would land right on top of Egyptian anti-aircraft batteries and armoured forces.

Eden was, according to the accounts of many later observers, already suffering under the stress of the situation, but on the morning of 2 November at the London meeting with the French generals he seemed on good form; one senior French commander entered the room to find the prime minister reclining on a sofa "looking distinguished" and chatting away in French – one of his several languages. Port Said itself was proving more of a problem as aerial reconnaissance showed dug-in defences.

Israeli paratroops undertaking training jumps.

The unpromising message to the chiefs of staff was that "the Egyptians are clearly going to resist our assault ... with everything they have got". Nasser had made an astute gamble. He was leaving the Israelis alone in the desert and waiting for Britain and France to put boots on the ground, an action that got more and more politically problematic the longer it was delayed.

World opinion was already making itself heard, even without aid from Moscow. Although there was support in some quarters, criticism quickly mounted against the British and French action. *The Sydney Morning Herald* proclaimed "Many, indeed even those who endorse Britain's policy, will be dismayed at her Government's rough disregard ... of her great American ally." The Pakistan *Dawn* newspaper was considerably less restrained. Under an editorial headlined "Hitler reborn" the British and French were taken to task. The paper declared they had

> suddenly turned the clock back hundreds of years, unwritten much of what has since been written in the book of human civilization, and decided to act as self-chartered libertines with the gun and the bomb, killing and conquering the weak like cowards.

Even British journalists were not especially inclined to be charitable. One covering the conflict from Cyprus for the *News Chronicle* reacted angrily when he was asked to refer to the campaign in terms other than 'war'. He confronted the commander of British forces on the island and told him, "I'm buggered if I'm going to call it a Police Action, I'm going to call it a war." In reply, the general told him "If you do, we'll hold up your reports forever." The general was true to his word and the journalist ended up giving up and returning to London.

The French had a more creative method of censoring negative news reports. The editor of *L'Express*, which immediately printed a series of anti-intervention articles, found himself called up as a military reservist and dispatched to Algeria.

# 14. RESOLUTION 997

Eisenhower was still in a rage. Even though the Suez Canal was now blocked – an action which halted oil supplies to Europe – he directly ordered government officials not to enact prearranged plans for emergency fuel shipments to Britain and France. One official recalled:

> The President said he was inclined to think that those who began this operation should be left to work out their own oil problems – to boil in their own oil, so to speak. They [the British] would be needing oil from Venezuela, and around the Cape, and before long they would be short of dollars to finance these operations and would be calling for help.

Dulles was also clear on the approach he thought should be adopted. At the National Security Council meeting on 1 November, he told his colleagues, "the United States has

A British ambulance being lowered from the deck to dockside during the Suez Crisis.

been walking a tightrope ... Unless we now assert and maintain American leadership ... We will be looked upon forever tied to British and French Colonialist policies." Britain and France were to be very publicly cast adrift.

The two "colonialist" allies did have one line of defence. They could veto any resolution proposed at the UN Security Council, just as Russia had vetoed the demand for Egypt to allow complete international control of the canal. But their line of defence was circumnavigated by the American representative at the UN, who moved for a resolution against the action taken at Suez in the full General Assembly, where no nation held veto power. The U.S.-instigated resolution began by "expressing its grave concern" at the Israeli invasion of Egypt, the interrupting of traffic through the Suez Canal and the military operations being conducted in Egyptian territory by the British and French. It then called for an immediate ceasefire, withdrawal of all forces to pre-war lines and the reopening of the canal. The central point was the statement that "all Member States refrain from introducing military goods in the area of hostilities"; in theory it called on every member state to get their military hardware out of the zone of conflict, but in reality it was a pointed demand to Britain and France to ground their planes and turn the amphibious force around.

On the evening of 2 November, the General Assembly voted. The resolution (997 ES-1) passed with a resounding sixty-four votes in favour and only five against. There were six abstentions. It was a brutal blow to Eden's attempts to maintain the front that British and French military action had any basis in international law. The day after the resolution passed at the UN, Eisenhower penned a letter to a high-school friend. His initial rage at being double-crossed had turned to pity.

> The real point is that Britain, France and Israel had come to believe – probably correctly – that Nasser was their worst enemy in the Middle East and that until he was removed or defeated, they would have no peace. I do not quarrel with the idea that there is justification for such fears, but I have insisted long and earnestly that you cannot resort to force in international relationships because of your fear of what might happen in the future.

Britain and France had now been publicly shamed at the UN, but there were few indications that UN's demand for a ceasefire would actually result in an end to the fighting, let alone resolve the crisis which now looked guaranteed to loom over Eisenhower's bid for re-election the following week. The twists and turns of the more than three-month-long Suez Crisis were already beginning to take their toll on participants. Dulles, who was utterly exhausted by the endless phone calls at all hours and the frantic dashing to and fro, was rushed into hospital in Washington on 3 November after he had woken with severe abdominal pain. He immediately went under the knife and surgeons found a cancerous tumour in his colon.

As the U.S. secretary of state was on his way to hospital, Eden began a televised address. He wore a dark suit with a white handkerchief poking out of the breast pocket, his grey hair was slicked back and he needed glasses to look down and read his notes. He began his address with a lie: "We have stepped in because the United Nations could not do so in time." He then added, in a statement that betrayed some unease, "If you see a fire, the first question is not how it started, but how to put it out", claiming that the British and French pounding of Nasser's military and its infrastructure was a "police action". He ended with a powerful statement of his own devoutly held convictions, clenching his fists next to his page of notes: "All my life I have been a man of peace, working for peace, striving for peace, negotiating for peace ... but I am utterly convinced that the action we have taken is right." It was a passionately held view that Eden would maintain, against all odds, for the rest of his life.

Eden was facing his own health troubles. The week before, as military action finally began, one Foreign Office official had remarked that the prime minister appeared "on the verge of a breakdown". The reality was worse. Eden had suffered from long-term stomach problems after a botched operation in 1953 severed his bile duct and early on in the crisis had found himself fighting off a recurring fever. As early as mid-August he had noted in his diary, "Felt rather wretched after a poor night. Awake 3.30 onwards with pain. Had to take pethidine [an opioid painkiller] in the end." Years later, he admitted in his memoirs "In early November ... [the doctor] who was taking care of me medically, began to be anxious at my state of health." Eden was exhausted. He had not taken a weekend off in months and it seemed his bile duct trouble was about to return with a vengeance. It was an awkward moment for any statesman to be ill.

On the night of Sunday, 4 November, Soviet troops attacked the Hungarian capital. While the occupants of the U.S. embassy sheltered in the basement, Henry Cabot Lodge, U.S. ambassador to the UN, addressed an emergency 3 a.m. session of the Security Council. He told representatives of the gathered nations, "We have just received word ... that Budapest is under heavy bombardment." Speaking over the radio to the sound of gunfire rattling in the background, Nagy stated:

> In the early hours of the morning, Soviet troops have started an attack against the Hungarian capital with the apparent purpose of overthrowing the lawful democratic government of the country. Our troops are engaged in battle ... This is my message to the Hungarian people and to the whole world.

By mid-morning, the Soviets had shut down radio transmissions, taken control of the parliament, the airfields and the bridges over the Danube. By the end of the day, refugees were streaming across the Hungarian border into Austria.

The situation in the U.S. State Department was one of complete paralysis. According to one official, "[everyone] was terribly distressed, considered ... what could be done, and really none of us had whatever imagination it took to discover another solution. We were just boxed in."

The problem was Suez. If the U.S. were to intervene to defend those denounced as aggressors, they would be forced to act against Britain and France. Eisenhower, in his address to the nation on the day Britain and France went to war, had clearly asserted, "We cannot, in the world, any more than in our own nation subscribe to one law for the weak, another for the strong; one law for those opposing us, another for those allied with us." The brutal summary of a CIA agent in Beirut was painfully accurate:

> The hollowness of American political rhetoric suddenly struck me ... trapped now by the perfidy of our own allies, we could do little but make speeches designed to encourage peoples who had taken the United States at its word.

As the first streaks of daylight appeared in the sky over Port Said on 5 November, the British and French finally prepared to put boots on the ground. The invasion armada was still a day away, but the amphibious force had swelled with the addition of the 430 Marines of 42 Commando who were crammed below decks on the carriers *Ocean* and *Theseus*, along with the helicopters that would transport them ashore.

Helicopters on the deck of HMS *Theseus*.

The commandos prepared for battle by camouflaging their dark webbing with hessian, dulling their cap badges and taping Sten submachine-gun magazines end to end, to enable them to reload faster in the heat of battle. On board, Peter Mayo questioned the eventual outcome of the operation, which he now knew was Suez, recording in his diary: "I wish I were happier about the cause we are to fight for ... where does it all lead?"

The parachute drops planned ahead of the amphibious assault had been delayed. Instead of arriving, as Ben-Gurion had anticipated, days after the Israelis had attacked, more than a week had passed. The delay was not a decision that went down well with the general in command of the French airborne troops, General Jean Gilles, who had previously been described by a British attaché as "the rudest, most unpleasant and most hostile French officer we have ever met". Eventually, the green light was given for the paras to drop on the morning of 5 November.

The 3rd Parachute Battalion was to land 668 men and seven jeeps, plus anti-tank guns, at Gamil airfield three miles west of Port Said. Simultaneously, the French 2nd Colonial Parachute Regiment would land on Port Fuad residential suburb on the east bank of the canal. Both drops greatly tested the skill of the paras. The British had to land on a tiny airfield 800 yards wide "surrounded by half-drained marshland", while the French had to hit a landing zone 300 yards long and 140 yards across. If they missed, they would end up in the canal or in trees. To make matters more interesting, their transport aircraft would have to fly in at 450 feet, around 200 feet less than the accepted minimum drop height. Some of the French airborne troops, who had seen action in Algeria and Indochina, were rather more experienced than their British counterparts. When one young English officer told a Frenchman he had done twenty-seven jumps, the bemused Frenchman replied that he had done three: French paras only counted the times they had actually jumped into action, not all their training jumps.

At 7:15 a.m. local time 3 Para leaped into action. The flight from Cyprus had been only ninety minutes. They jumped without reserve parachutes, as carrying a spare 'chute at the drop height of 600 feet would have been a pointless exercise anyway. Gamil airfield was taken quickly, with only four dead and thirty-six wounded.

One of those injured was the regimental medical officer, who lost an eye. In Cyprus, there were no parachute-trained doctors to go and replace him, so the three air force doctors drew lots for who would have to jump in. In the event, the medical officer was patched up and carried on, later being awarded a Military Cross.

The French also swiftly secured their objective of the Raswa bridges which linked Port Said and Suez, demonstrating great professionalism in nailing their landing zone and completing the operation in an hour and a half, well ahead of schedule.

For Nasser, the military situation was now verging on a disaster. Instead of an orderly withdrawal from the Sinai, many Egyptian soldiers had simply abandoned their equipment and fled. An Egyptian Army major later narrated:

Paras from the 3rd Battalion land at El Gamil airfield.

> There was mile after mile [of] Egyptian armour on the road [from Cairo] and every truck and armoured vehicle was burning after the air attacks ... poor farmers were walking on the road and screaming at us: "You have brought this destruction on our land."

The president called on Egyptian citizens to carry on the war against the invaders – "We shall fight a bitter battle ... from village to village, house to house" – and began distributing small arms among the general population. In practical terms, despite the arrival of British and French forces on the ground, fighting was almost ended. The Israelis had secured the Sinai and had halted within ten miles of the canal itself. The waterway was unusable, but it was hardly under threat and the Egyptians were no longer really fighting. There was no war for the British and French to wade in as "police" to stop anymore.

Eden and his Cabinet met twice in one day to discuss their response to the UN resolution. They arrived at the solution that British forces would basically ignore the UN-demanded ceasefire, suggesting they could play a role separating the combatants until a suitably equipped UN peacekeeping force arrived. Eden sent Eisenhower an almost apologetic note:

> I am convinced that, if we had allowed things to drift ... Nasser would have become a kind of Muslim Mussolini ... We and the French were convinced that we had to act ... we must go on to hold the position until we can hand over responsibility to the United Nations.

## Resolution 997

The Israelis lost some of their armour, such as this knocked-out Sherman tank, but many Egyptian vehicles were simply abandoned.

Troops of 3rd Battalion, The Parachute Regiment escort a captured Egyptian soldier.

British troops distribute food in Port Said, 12 November 1956.

When the policy was announced in the Commons, Eden faced an onslaught of abuse from the Opposition benches during a specially called Saturday sitting. Eden still had the support of his own party members, but ended up walking from the chamber as the session adjourned to shouts of "Resign!" from the benches opposite.

On 5 November, mounted police charged anti-war demonstrators who had congregated near the Cenotaph war memorial in Whitehall. The day before, more than 20,000 had gathered to protest in Trafalgar Square. A U.S. diplomat in London who witnessed the Trafalgar Square protests later recalled:

> [there was] a depth of feeling on the part of young university students, of old manual workers, and of many ages and classes in between that I had not realized existed in Britain. The vast majority was loudly and passionately opposed to Eden and his Middle East policy.

# 15. ELECTION DAY

Dulles was in hospital recovering from the surgery to remove the tumour from his colon, but he was still working and Macmillan spent the early hours of the morning of 6 November on the phone with the secretary of state. Macmillan's problem was money. Even on the eve of British and French military action, Macmillan had warned the Cabinet that U.S. dollar reserves were "falling at a dangerously rapid rate". He added, "in view of the extent to which we might have to rely on American economic assistance," Britain "could not afford to alienate the U.S. Government any more than was absolutely necessary." Initially Macmillan had been one of the most hawkish members of Eden's Cabinet, but as the military campaign got underway he began to change his tune. The difficult reality was that the Americans did not just feel alienated, they felt completely deceived and by the start of November, 15 per cent of British gold and dollar reserves had evaporated. Dulles was blunt with Macmillan over the phone. The U.S. would only help prop up sterling if Britain agreed to the UN ceasefire.

Eden was also up and working. He was woken at 2 a.m. by the arrival of the message addressed to him from Bulganin. The Russian premier threatened the use of "rocket weapons" against Britain and France, adding, "We are fully determined to crush the aggressors by the use of force and to restore peace in the East." When the Cabinet

The long-awaited landing at Port Said began on the morning of 6 November.

convened at 9:45 a.m. that morning they had to deal with both the threat of nuclear war and the threat of economic collapse.

Five hours before an increasingly tired-looking Eden took the chair at Cabinet, the curtain rose on the final act of *Musketeer*. At 6 a.m. Egyptian time, destroyers opened fire on installations in Port Said harbour, as Royal Marines clambered into their landing craft. Ahead of them, swooping fighters strafed the beaches until two minutes before the landing craft arrived. The marines on *Theseus* and *Ocean* prepared to go into battle by helicopter for the first time, but the short journey was a precarious one: the Whirlwinds had no seats or doors and almost nothing to hold on to inside. The helicopters lifted off from the decks of the carriers just after the first wave had landed on the beach.

The chosen helicopter landing point was on the Port Said waterfront, rather appropriately close to a proud statue of de Lesseps, which had been erected in honour of the canal's architect. As the helicopters took off from HMS *Ocean*, one marine recalled, "We were barely two or three miles off shore and roughly in line with the mouth of the Canal. The skyline was dominated by an immense plume of heavy black smoke ... A fringe of flame seemed to lick from the beach itself." The strange lull ended quickly. "The shoreline rushed up towards us before I had time to think ... We

Westland Whirlwinds taking off from HMS *Theseus*.

*Election Day*

Israeli generals Haim Laskov, Moshe Kashti, Asaf Simchoni and Dan Tolkovski in the Sinai.

descended into a whirling, choking, blinding cloud of white dust ... I could see nothing, but as I felt the bump, I leapt as bravely and as purposefully as I could manage, out into the dust cloud."

Another of the helicopter-deployed marines landed in complete blindness on the sandy beach. Through the haze he discerned a figure above him who appeared hostile. It turned out to be his brigade's military assistant who was part of the group which had already occupied the beach. "How nice to see you here, Nick." he casually remarked. "I think if you get your chaps up and walk to the road, you'll find everybody else is waiting for you." With the support of Centurion tanks, British forces fought to take control of the harbour, largely encountering only concentrated pockets of Egyptian resistance.

The experience of finally coming under fire was surreal for Peter Mayo:

Bullets were still flying, some whickering past high-up, and some nearer with that venomous crack. For some reason I found myself walking along quite casually, having got, I suppose, into a frame mind of where, not actually seeing who was shooting at us, one didn't believe the bullets were actually aimed at oneself personally.

In a remarkably unchoreographed move, British and French forces finally linked up outside the offices of the Suez Canal Company.

A British Centurion tank of the 6th Royal Tank Regiment disembarks from an LST (landing ship, tank) at Port Said.

At Downing Street, the mood in Cabinet was sombre. Bulganin's threatening overnight message to Eden was being taken seriously and a number of ministers expressed concern that if they carried on the military operation then Soviet forces might intervene; the Joint Intelligence Committee had received reports the Russians were preparing to mobilize aircraft to attack.

Macmillan then told the Cabinet that Britain's dollar reserves had been depleted by one-eighth in the previous week alone, a fall of $280 million. (It later transpired that Macmillan got his sums wrong – the fall was in fact closer to $135 million – and he may either have made a howling error, or been deliberately ramping up the economic pressure having changed his mind about military action.) The devaluation of sterling and a run on the pound was now a looming prospect. Macmillan, previously so forcefully for war, said to his colleagues, "in view of the financial and economic pressures, we must stop."

Eden still wished to press on, but the vast majority of his Cabinet did not. Lloyd was among the critics. He told his colleagues it was "urgently necessary that we should regain the initiative by bringing hostilities to an end". The gradual build-up of international, financial and domestic pressure had finally broken the resolve of the British politicians

Port Said viewed from the air.

in the Cabinet. With even Macmillan demanding a halt to operations, time had run out for Eden. He caved to the Cabinet's decision. Eden personally telephoned Guy Mollet to break the news.

The French prime minister was pulled out of a meeting with the German chancellor to take the call. Eden got straight to the point: "I don't think we can go on. The pressure on sterling is becoming unbearable. The English can take a lot of things, but I do not think they would be willing to accept the failure of sterling." Mollet pleaded for another three days, but Eden was sadly adamant. "No," he replied, "I cannot hold out any longer." His country's finances, its ministers' appetite for war and Eden's own body were all reaching the end of their limit. After a brief moment, the French prime minister passed the phone to his foreign secretary. Pineau later recalled, "I heard the broken voice of a man who was at the end of his tether and ready to let himself sink."

As Eden was guiltily phoning Mollet and Pineau, Dayan was watching the Star of David being run up a flagpole above the Red Sea resort of Sharm el-Sheikh on the southern tip of the desert. He noted in his diary it was

# Suez Crisis 1956

Moshe Dayan (third from the right) salutes the raising of the Star of David at Sharm el-Sheikh, 6 November 1956.

One of the most spectacular views I have ever seen. Its waters are deep blue (Egyptian prisoners warned us against swimming there for they are teeming with sharks) and they are framed by hills of crimson rock.

It marked a resounding victory for the Israelis, who had achieved their aim of seeing the threat of the Egyptian military annihilated, while also taking complete control of the Sinai. Several thousand Egyptians had been killed and a further 5,600 taken prisoner for the loss of only 171 Israeli lives.

Sharm el-Sheikh had proved difficult to capture: the town had only been taken after two days of airstrikes in which Israeli jets used napalm to try and clear out the defenders. Dayan read out a letter from Ben-Gurion to the hundreds of assembled Israeli soldiers.

When Israel's prime minister later addressed the Knesset he was a in a triumphant mood. He quoted Procopius – the Roman historian he had been reading on the flight to Sèvres – and delighted in asserting that an island off Sharm el-Sheikh had been a Hebrew-controlled port in the time of King Solomon; it was simply being returned to its rightful owner. "This was the greatest and most glorious military operation in the annals of our people," he declared, adding, "all their modern arms and equipment were of no avail … and the words of the prophet Isaiah were fulfilled: 'In that day shall Egypt tremble and be afraid.'"

Egyptian prisoners of war at a PoW camp in Israel.

As part of Dayan's address at Sharm el-Sheikh, he read out a letter from Ben-Gurion.

A few hours after Dayan had watched the emotional flag-raising over Sharm el-Sheikh, Eisenhower received his election-morning briefing from the CIA. He ordered U-2 flights to check on Soviet aircraft in Syria to make sure they had not moved, admitting to the men in the room, "If the Soviets should attack Britain and France directly, we would of course be in a major war." Eisenhower then travelled home to Pennsylvania to cast his own vote in the election, before meeting with the Joint Chiefs of Staff and the CIA at midday. To show Bulganin that he was serious that the U.S. would still stand by Britain in the event of Soviet attack, he ordered air defences to be put on alert, approved the sailing of two extra aircraft carriers to join the Azores fleet, recalled all U.S. military personnel from leave and put strategic nuclear forces on alert. It was a series of actions designed to make the Kremlin take notice. In the middle of the meeting, Eisenhower put through a call to Eden.

Eden informed him, "We cease firing tonight at midnight."

Eisenhower's reply was smooth and cheerful: "I can't tell you how pleased we are."

They went on to discuss Eden's imminent appearance in Parliament where Eden would face a vote of no confidence. Eden unemotionally stated, "If I survive here tonight I will call you tomorrow." (Eden went on to win the vote that night, although six of his own MPs abstained.) Before he rang off, Eden asked after the election. "We have given our whole thought to Hungary and the Middle East," Eisenhower replied, "I don't give a damn how the election goes. I guess it will be all right."

Destroyed Egyptian guns at Sharm el-Sheikh.

## Election Day

In Port Said, the last resistance had finally been extinguished as darkness fell. The overall commander of Anglo-French ground forces, General Sir Hugh Stockwell, had just finished touring the captured port and arrived back at the fleet to receive the order to ceasefire. He later recalled:

> We were on the verge of complete success ... By Thursday night we surely would have been down to Suez ... Now, just as we were reaping the reward of all the effort and the months of preparation, we were to be thwarted of our prize.

A significant number of serving personnel at Suez found out about the ceasefire from that evening's BBC news.

There were victorious scenes in Washington and Moscow that night. Eisenhower won a second term with a landslide victory and 57 per cent of the vote. In his address he promised, "With whatever talents the good God has given me, with whatever strength there is within me" to "work for 168 million Americans here at home – and for peace in the world."

Khrushchev was of the oversimplified view that the threat of starting of nuclear war was what had forced Eden to cave, even though the Politburo had never intended to follow through. He claimed the simple fact was that "twenty-four hours after the delivery of our note the aggression was halted". He gleefully told the Egyptian ambassador, "You have cut off the British lion's tail and we have drawn his teeth!"

# 16. BLACK GOLD AND BLUE HELMETS

The announcement of the ceasefire, though cathartic, did nothing to solve the economic problems Britain faced. The blocking of the Suez Canal had the effect that had been prophesied and the government moved to reduce oil consumption as demand outstripped supply and prices rose. The knock-on impact of going to war was that Saudi Arabia halted oil exports to Britain; the country was fast losing all its allies in the Middle East. Dollar and gold reserves fell below the Bank of England's designated minimum level of $2,000 million and it was expected that when the next announcement of reserves figures was required to be made – 3 December – the news of the drop would further add to the flight from sterling. Britain would need a supporting loan from the International Monetary Fund, but to get it, they would have to secure help from Washington. The alternative was unthinkable. The pound would have to move to a floating rate against the dollar which in the words of one official would "be a catastrophe ... [for] the cost of living and [the] level of wages in this country". It would also shatter international confidence in the British economy.

The secret of Sèvres – already speculated on in the U.S. press – was now less secret than it had ever been after Mollet had practically admitted something along those lines had happened in a spectacular slip-up at a press conference. Ten days after the ceasefire had been declared, Pineau met up with the recovering Dulles for lunch. The Frenchman confided in his American opposite number the entire plan. Dulles remembered, "He, in effect, apologized for not having kept us informed."

Since 11 November, Lloyd had been doing the rounds across 'The Pond' trying to salvage Britain's battered reputation, but to no avail. At an Organization for European Economic Cooperation (OEEC) meeting on 15 November, Macmillan approached U.S. officials and tried to discuss the redirection of oil supplies. He was rebuffed, as at NSC meetings it had already been decided that there would be no change on the policy of strangling Britain's oil while British troops remained in Egypt. Before the war had broken out, Macmillan had said to the Cabinet, "If we lose the Middle East, we lose the oil. If we lose the oil, we cannot live." Months later, his prediction was coming perilously close to being fulfilled.

Eden's health was now in a dire state and his doctor ordered him to rest. On 19 November he was forced to cancel all engagements. The next day, *The Times* reported he was "suffering from the effects of severe overstrain". In his memoirs Eden wrote, "after consultation with my principal colleagues, I acquiesced in a decision to go for a few weeks to Jamaica." Eden was visibly seriously ill, but the decision to leave the country at a crucial juncture played extremely badly. Churchill's private secretary noted, "With petrol and oil rationed again in England, the retreat of the Prime Minister to a ... paradise seemed to rank prominently in the annals of ministerial follies." On 23 November, Eden and his wife flew to the Caribbean. The decision was a gift to Eden's critics. The *Daily Mirror* ran a competition offering readers a three-week holiday in Jamaica as a prize for a 200-word "solution" to the Suez Crisis. The holiday went to a young woman who suggested Britain should bow to the will of the UN. The James Bond novelist Ian Fleming lent Eden and his wife Clarissa his villa on the north coast of the island. While the couple were there, they planted a Santa Maria tree, which has flourished and now grown to a height of over 100 feet. In the words of one commentator, the tree was "perhaps the only good thing to have come out of the Suez debacle".

Four days before Eden left for Jamaica and before *The Times* had publicized that the prime minister was suffering "overstrain" Macmillan popped around to the London residence of the U.S. ambassador. He told him that Eden "Will have to go on vacation immediately, first for one week and then for another, and this will lead to his retirement." The writing was on the wall.

In Eden's absence, the Cabinet agreed to a complete withdrawal of British forces in Egypt. A sheepish Lloyd confirmed the decision in Parliament on 3 December, claiming rather fancifully, "We have stopped a small war and prevented a large one." The new reality was clear: "Responsibility for securing a settlement of the long-term problems of the area has now been placed squarely on the shoulders of the United Nations." In short, the once-imperial power was running away, her tail between her legs.

Discussions about "the money" through diplomatic channels had cleared the way for what happened next. Within three days, oil was shipping out of the Gulf of Mexico to European ports; the U.S. supported Britain's formal request to draw down an eyewatering $561 million from the IMF, with a further $738 million reserve, which was formalized on 10 December. The question marks hanging over the future value of sterling were dismissed, but others remained. *The Economist* noted, "As the dust swirls over the Middle East ... there is only one subject in domestic politics. It is the Prime Minister – should he go or stay?"

Eden returned from Jamaica looking tanned and rested on 14 December. Before boarding the plane he had spoken to journalists and told them, "I am assured that on my return to this country I shall feel completely fit – ready to resume my duties at once." But his political health was now as pressing a consideration. Eden was straight back into the fray. At the airport he determinedly told the press: "I am convinced, more convinced than I have been about anything in all my public life, that we were right ... and that history will prove it so." Soon afterwards he faced hostile questioning in Parliament over the road to war. The narrative of police action was, he was told, "no longer credible and is no longer believed"; even *The Times* was now publishing letters alleging collusion between the British, the French and Israelis. In response Eden simply lied in the House of Commons. "[To say] that Her Majesty's Government were engaged in some dishonourable conspiracy is completely untrue, and I most emphatically deny it." Eden went to his grave never admitting the collusion that had taken Britain and France to war.

There were still 13,500 British and 8,500 French troops in Port Said, along with thousands of vehicles and all their supplies. Their position was a difficult one, described by one chief of staff in no uncertain terms as "a toe hold in Egypt". A significant number of men were stuck on ships while the ones ashore faced their own difficulties. The occupying forces came under occasional sniper fire when driving through the streets and were targeted with grenades lobbed from upper-floor windows. The French in particular did not endear themselves to the local population. One Egyptian canal pilot remembered:

> The British were well behaved – they did not steal anything when they were billeted in my apartment. But the French behaviour was very different. They treated people very badly. Maybe it was their experience of Algeria but I think they were angry because they thought the canal belonged to them and that they had a right to take it back.

For the British and French in Port Said, staying or leaving was, the staff officer noted, "a most ghastly administrative problem".

The composition of the UN force which would deploy to replace the British and French and ensure everyone returned to their pre-war lines was hotly contested. Nasser refused to have any soldiers who even remotely looked British or French and on that basis flatly

Withdrawing the thousands of soldiers and all their equipment and stores was not a simple task.

objected to the deployment of Canadians. He did however welcome the force, as they provided a buffer between his devastated military and the victorious Israeli forces. The Egyptian leader used the canal as his bargaining chip: "So long as there is a foreign force, one single foreign soldier in Egypt, we shall not begin repairing the Canal and we shall not begin running the Canal."

The French had already agreed to leave and the Americans insisted the British – despite protestations that they wished to take part – were not welcome. The result was that the troops who arrived came from Denmark, Finland, India, Indonesia, Norway and Sweden. There was no UN uniform, so to distinguish the peacekeepers it was suggested they should wear berets in the distinctive blue of the UN flag. In the absence of specially made headgear they improvised, spray-painting U.S.-made plastic helmet-liners.

On 22 November, the first 'blue helmets' arrived in Port Said. Marine Peter Mayo noted in his diary, "The [Egyptian] crowd was cheering the Norwegians and at the same time shaking their fists at the British troops."

The full withdrawal took several weeks and the invaders departed with a number of trophies of war, the French taking furniture and a clock which had been given to de Lesseps from the Suez Canal Company offices on the Port Said waterfront. The canal itself was completely blocked. The Egyptians had sunk fifty-one wrecks in the waterway and its approaches in Port Said harbour and had proved most creative in their choice of obstacles: there were floating cranes, tugs, pilot boats and even a frigate firmly settled on the bottom. Suez did not re-open to shipping for nearly four months.

For many serving personnel, the enforced departure was a bitter blow to morale. The moment and indeed the Suez Crisis itself was summed up by one melancholy British civil servant, who noted in his diary, "all the Services feel they have been betrayed, and that we will never be able to show any independence as a nation again ... Petrol is up by one and sixpence."

Nasser welcomed the arrival of UN troops, although not Canadians.

# EPILOGUE: THE CURSE OF THE PHARAOHS

On 23 December 1956, the last British troops left Port Said. On Christmas Eve, a jubilant throng assembled on the dockside, next to the thirty-three-foot bronze statue of Ferdinand de Lesseps that had been erected in the Frenchman's honour in 1899. A ring of explosives was set around the base and detonated and the architect of the Suez Canal came tumbling down. All that was left was his boots. It was a fitting metaphor for the end of British and French imperialism in Egypt.

A few weeks later, Anthony Eden resigned as prime minister and as a member of parliament. He had lost the confidence of his Cabinet and his doctors had advised him that his body could no longer bear the strain anyway. The unspoken truth was that it was the Suez Crisis that had brought about his downfall. Before he departed, two junior officials in the Foreign Office were ordered to put together a file of all the sensitive documents relating to the crisis and to deliver it to the Cabinet secretary. Just like the British copy of the Sèvres Protocol, the incriminating papers were never seen again.

On 18 January 1957, Eden and his wife set sail from a fog-shrouded Tilbury docks to holiday in New Zealand. The cruise liner's voyage took longer than usual, as the RMS *Rangitata* had to sail via the Panama Canal, because Suez was still closed. Nasser was

Despite the Suez Crisis being a military defeat, Nasser's popularity soared following the crisis.

## Epilogue: The Curse of the Pharaohs

the undisputed victor, even though his armies had lost every battle; the French paper *Le Monde* dejectedly declared, "The prestige of Colonel Nasser in the Arab countries has never been greater." Egypt's leader had no sympathy for the vanquished, as one Egyptian journalist recalled: "he never felt one speck of pity for Eden" and when Eden resigned Nasser remarked, "It was the Curse of the Pharaohs." In October the following year, the Egyptian leader struck a deal with the Soviets for the financing of the Aswan Dam.

The departure of the British and French left a Cold War vacuum in the Middle East. Dulles noted in a meeting to discuss the fallout from the Suez Crisis, "We must now take over the burden of the British and French in dealing with Nasser." When he debated the broader regional picture with Eisenhower as the last British troops were leaving, he told the president:

> If we do not act, the Soviets are likely to take over the area and they could thereby control Europe through oil on which Europe is dependent ... We must fill the vacuum of power which the British filled for a century.

The result was the creation of the 'Eisenhower Doctrine', which was revealed on 5 January 1957. Eisenhower outlined to Congress the "increased danger from International Communism" in the Middle East and requested approval for programmes of economic and military support, as well as authorization to deploy troops "to secure and protect the territorial integrity and political independence of such nations". The Cold War showed no signs of abating.

A decade later, the U.S. found itself entangled in the former French colony of Indochina, ramping up military support against Communist guerrillas. Lyndon Johnson's administration made discreet inquiries for British assistance in Vietnam, but the response was clear. The reply from Downing Street asserted, "The Prime Minister [then Labour's Harold Wilson] would have great difficulty in the Commons. Most members of Parliament think Washington is morally in the wrong." Almost as an afterthought it was noted, "And many remember the American reaction to Suez." The Suez Crisis was above all a watershed moment for Britain's place in the world, but it was also the moment of greatest rift in the 'special relationship'. As Khrushchev remarked, the U.S. helped their allies "the way the rope helps the man who is hanged".

Ben-Gurion's glee over the capture of the Sinai was short lived. Washington insisted in no uncertain terms that they evacuate, which the Israelis did in the spring of 1957. The embarrassment inflicted on the Egyptian military also backfired, as it was a factor in pushing Nasser into an even more militaristic anti-Israeli stance, which stoked regional tension that led to another Arab-Israeli conflict in 1967. Moshe Dayan was by then minister of defence and directed Israeli operations in the Six-Day War.

The Israeli Air Force – equipped with newer French-made aircraft – conducted a pre-emptive strike on Egyptian forces. When Egyptian ground troops entered the Sinai,

## Suez Crisis 1956

Israeli troops leaving Suez.

pushing aside the UN's thin blue line of peacekeepers which Nasser had denounced as "a force serving neo-imperialism", they did so having already handed complete air superiority to their foe. The brief conflict resulted in a remarkable victory for the Israelis. Nasser resigned but reversed his decision after protestors supporting him took to the streets of Cairo. He died in office three years later, a diminished figure.

For Mollet and Pineau, Suez was not the personal catastrophe that it was for Eden. France turned inward to Europe, signing the Treaty of Rome, one of the founding charters of the European Union, in March 1957, while research began to secretly develop the country's own nuclear deterrent. But the conflict in Algeria haunted both men and years of horrific violence and the rising cost of the war were instrumental in bringing down not just their administration, but the entire Fourth Republic. In its place, the French wartime leader Charles de Gaulle took power with the support of the military.

Khrushchev was the longest lived of the Suez-era leaders, the Soviet premier holding power until the machinations within the Politburo eventually led to his removal in 1964. Before being ousted he played a central role in the Cuban Missile Crisis – the closest East and West ever came to an all-out nuclear war. Hungary, meanwhile, suffered under the rule of a Soviet-installed leader who presided over a wave of arrests and executions of those involved in the 1956 uprising, among them Imre Nagy, who was hanged.

The Suez Crisis had the greatest impact on Britain; it became the first, but not the last time the nation's leaders deceived the country into going to war. The crisis came to

*Epilogue: The Curse of the Pharaohs*

Israeli forces secured a swift victory in the Six-Day War.

The Egyptian Air Force was again obliterated on the ground ten years after Suez during the 1967 Six-Day War with Israel.

The destruction of the de Lesseps statue made front-page news in Cairo.

represent not simply an example of a badly bungled battle in a foreign land, but a more deep-seated question about Britain's place in the world. After the crisis, one of Dulles's predecessors as secretary of state famously remarked, "Great Britain has lost an empire and has not yet found a role." Britain's position as a major player in the Middle East was in tatters. Swept up in the tide of post-Suez Arab nationalism, King Hussein abrogated the Anglo-Jordanian Treaty and threatened to get the money needed to prop up his administration from Egypt and the Saudis; it was the Americans that stumped up a gift of $10 million which brought him back into the pro-Western fold and since 1956 it has been Washington that has, for good or ill, been the predominant player "east of Suez".

Anthony Eden has been much vilified for his role in the Suez Crisis, but despite the manifest delusions he carried with him to his grave, the effect of the crisis on foreign policy was not lost on the man who had dealt with Britain's overseas affairs for most of his political career. In the shadow of the crisis, shortly before he left office, Eden penned a revealing memorandum to the colleagues who would gladly usurp him. He noted, "We must review our world position and our domestic capacity more searchingly in the light of the Suez experience, which has not so much changed our fortunes as revealed realities."

# AFTERWORD: THE PARALLELS OF SUEZ AND IRAQ

Mass anti-war protests in Trafalgar Square, a British prime minister desperate to see the downfall of a Middle Eastern dictator and a plot to take a nation to war that goes to the heart of government: it is not difficult to find easy parallels between the Suez Crisis of 1956 and the invasion of Iraq in 2003. Two years after the war began, as Iraq descended into bloody chaos, *The Times* ran an article under the headline "Suez and Iraq, two of a kind", adding "the ironies are uncanny". Such comparisons are tempting to make and play into the notion that "history repeats itself", in no small part because we never learn from it. However, while there are a number of intriguing parallels between the two, the Iraq war in many ways demonstrated the lasting impact of the Suez Crisis on the psyche of British politicians and public forty-seven years on.

In a passionate speech at the Labour Party conference in 2001 which the British prime minister had drafted himself, Tony Blair declared, "The kaleidoscope has been shaken, the pieces are in flux, soon they will settle again. Before they do let us reorder this world around us."* The terror attacks on the World Trade Centre in New York a month before were, for Blair, a watershed moment. The response was the invasion of Afghanistan, the hideout of Osama bin Laden, the mastermind of 9/11. Less logically, came the wider extension of the "war on terror". The dictatorial regime of Saddam Hussein's Iraq, which had already fought one war with America and Britain in 1991 after an international coalition responded to counteract Saddam's invasion of oil-rich Kuwait, was now in the firing line.

This time, the pressure for immediate war came not from Paris, but from Washington. U.S. President George W. Bush named Iraq as part of an "axis of evil" and it soon became clear that the Bush administration intended action to follow. At a meeting of Cabinet on 28 February 2002, Blair's ministers discussed the speculation that the Bush administration sought a war in Iraq. Robin Cook, the leader of the House of Commons who would later resign over the decision to invade, stated that action "will not be supported in Europe". Most Arab leaders, he added, would say that the greatest menace in the Middle East was not Saddam Hussein, but Israel's hard-line leader Ariel Sharon. Cook's comment on Sharon – the man who had led Israel's 202 Brigade in support of the Israeli paratroops landed in the Mitla Pass in 1956 – got a round of 'hear hears' at the table, "the nearest I've heard to a mutiny in the Cabinet", Cook later noted in his diary.†

---

\* Michael White, 'Let us reorder this world', *The Guardian*, 3 October 2001.
† Andy McSmith, 'Chilcot Report: The inside story of how Tony Blair led Britain to war in Iraq', *Independent*, 4 July 2016.

Ariel Sharon, a military commander in 1956, went on to become Israel's prime minister; pictured here meeting with French leader Jacques Chirac.

The narrative in favour of war was twofold, based on American claims that the plotters of 9/11 had links to Iraqi intelligence and that Saddam Hussein, contrary to his assertions, was developing weapons of mass destruction which represented a threat to the wider world and a "clear and present danger" to the West. The 'Sèvres moment' for Iraq was Saturday, 6 April 2002, at a private pre-dinner meeting between U.S. Vice-President Dick Cheney and Tony Blair at a ranch in Crawford, Texas. There, it is claimed, Blair promised that if the U.S. invaded Iraq, Britain would go along as well. It was a commitment not just to action, but to regime change. Britain's ambassador to the U.S., who was not in the meeting, but who stayed at the ranch at the time, later stated their "convergence" was "signed in blood at the Crawford ranch."*

The perspective in Baghdad was not unlike that in Cairo. Saddam could only watch and wait to be invaded. In that regard, Nasser at least was in far greater control of his own destiny and, due to his fence-sitting position on the Cold War, had the prospect of a diplomatic and face-saving solution, as neither Russia nor the United States wanted the Suez Crisis to be the trigger for the Cold War to turn hot. There was no such opportunity

---

\* 'Iraq inquiry: Tony Blair "agreed to regime change in meeting at George Bush's ranch", *Daily Telegraph*, 26 November 2009.

## Afterword: The Parallels of Suez and Iraq

Tony Blair and George W. Bush.

for Saddam who was already an international pariah. The Iraqi leader was very aware of the march of events. In an interview in February 2003, eight weeks before bombs began to fall on Baghdad, he insisted:

> No Iraqi official or ordinary citizen has expressed a wish to go to war ... If the purpose was to make sure that Iraq is free of nuclear, chemical and biological weapons then they can do that ... It is in our interest to facilitate their mission to find the truth. The question is, does the other side want to get to the same conclusion or are they looking for a pretext for aggression?[*]

As in the case of Suez, the move which preceded war was to take the problem to the UN. The result was resolution 1441 which warned that Iraq "will face serious consequences as a result of continued violations of its obligations [regarding weapons of mass destruction]" and handed the Iraqi government "a final opportunity to comply with its disarmament

---
[*] Mcah L. Sifry and Christopher Cerf (ed.), *The Iraqi War Reader, History, Documents, Opinions*, Touchstone, 2003, p. 464.

regulations" to prove it had given up attempts to develop nuclear, chemical and biological weapons; Saddam had used chemical weapons against Iran in the two nations' brutal conflict between 1980 and 1988, but subsequently insisted stockpiles had been destroyed and all research halted. The UN resolution clearly did not support the use of force, but in the absence of any definitive legal backing it became expedient to try and prove that it did not prohibit it.

Eden faced votes of confidence in Parliament over the decision to go to war, while Blair sought the approval of MPs before committing British forces. He passionately claimed that Iraq was in breach of resolution 1441, presenting a now-infamous dossier that allegedly evidenced that Iraq's weapons programme was still ongoing. Speaking in the House of Commons ahead of a crucial division that was secured with only 149 votes against compared to 412 in favour, Blair painted himself as Eden had in the wake of the UN deliberations. He claimed the reason for waiting was

> because resolution 1441 gave a final opportunity … But still we waited. We waited for the inspectors' reports. We waited as each concession was tossed to us to whet our appetite for hope and further waiting. But still no one, not even today at the Security Council, says that Saddam is co-operating fully.

Just as Eden had, Blair also invoked the demons of the past: "The tragedy is that the world has to learn the lesson all over again that weakness in the face of a threat from a tyrant is the surest way not to peace, but – unfortunately – to conflict." He then read out a letter written after Chamberlain's Munich Agreement in 1938 that claimed Britain was safe and added, "Now, of course, should Hitler again appear in the same form we would know what to do. But the point is that history does not declare the future to us plainly."* Forty-seven years before the threat had been Mussolini on the Nile, now it was Hitler on the Tigris. Two days later, the war in Iraq began.

As with Suez, the immediate military campaign in Iraq was a success – Saddam fell within weeks – but the aftermath proved more difficult. In the case of Iraq, the removal of Saddam's heavy-handed rule unleashed suppressed ethnic and religious strife which was ruthlessly exploited by different factions and instead of ushering in an era of peaceful democracy, the invasion was the precursor to a devastating civil war. Only in recent years has Iraq begun to witness some semblance of stability, but the scars will take many decades to heal.

For Blair, the Iraq war was a political nightmare. There were no weapons of mass destruction and the claims that had swung the vote were proved false. The fallout dragged on and Blair eventually resigned in 2007, two years after winning a third term on a much-diminished majority. In his resignation speech, he listed his domestic achievements in office, but all were eclipsed, and remain so, by the Iraq war. Like Suez for Eden, Iraq became Blair's only lasting legacy.

---

\* Hansard, Commons Debates, 18 March 2003, 'Iraq'.

*Afterword: The Parallels of Suez and Iraq*

F. The Royal Navy minesweeper HMS *Bossington* (M1133) during operations in the Suez Canal, January 1974.

There was never any inquiry into the Suez Crisis, but there was one into the 2003 Iraq war. The lengthy Chilcot Report was finally published in 2016, seven years after the inquiry's announcement by Gordon Brown, Blair's successor as prime minister. Blair's response to the unsurprising findings was contrition, but not for the war itself. He apologized for the failures of planning that had plunged Iraq into violence, telling journalists "I express more sorrow, regret and apology than you can ever know or believe" but went on to insist that he still believed that action to remove Saddam Hussein was correct. In words that remarkably parallel Eden's on his return to London from Jamaica in December 1956, Blair said, "I did it because I thought it was right."*

If there is a parallel between Suez and Iraq, it is not to be found in the war itself or the tangled road to a costly conflict. It is in the two men who led Britain to war under false pretences. Like Eden, Blair wrote his own self-selective memoir in which he painted his version of events with messianic fervour. In it he asserted:

> the argument [over the Iraq war] raged fiercely back then and rages fiercely today. History, as ever, will be the final judge. At this point, I don't seek agreement. I seek merely an understanding that the arguments for and against were more balanced than conventional wisdom suggests. This was not Suez.†

---

\* Rowena Mason, Anushka Asthana and Heather Stewart, 'Tony Blair: "I express more sorrow, regret and apology thank you can ever believe"', *The Guardian*, 6 July 2016.
† Tony Blair, *A Journey*, Arrow Books, 2011, p. 391.

# SOURCES

## THE DISAPPEARING EVIDENCE
Even though a batch of incriminating Suez papers disappeared at Eden's request – presumably going the way of the Sèvres Protocol in the Cabinet secretary's fireplace – much material remains. Further newly declassified British documents were released in 2007, but the brutal truth is that there are few secrets of the Suez Crisis left to hide, given that the British and French collusion with the Israelis was exposed so quickly. The British copy of the protocol was burned and the French version filed away and 'lost', but the Israeli document became publicly available in 1996 and a copy is now even held in the Public Records Office.

Eden's secret 1952 memorandum in which he stated he wished the canal to become an area of "international responsibility" can be found at the National Archives in Kew under CAB 129/53, entitled 'Britain's Overseas Obligations' dated 18 June of that year. His final note – that Suez had revealed the "realities" of Britain's position in the world – was penned in December 1956 under the heading 'Thoughts', see PRO, PREM 11/1138.

## SELECT ANNOTATED BIBLIOGRAPHY
Ambrose, Stephen, *Eisenhower, The President*, Vol II, Simon and Schuster, 1984.
Ashton, Nigel (ed.), *The Cold War in the Middle East*, Routledge, 2007.
Barker, A. J., *Suez: The Seven Day War*, Faber and Faber, 1964.
Bar-Zohar, *Ben-Gurion*, Weidenfeld and Nicholson, 1978.
Brendon, Piers, *The Decline and Fall of the British Empire*, Random House, 2010.
Barry, Turner, *Suez 1956*, Hodder & Stoughton, 2006 provides a detailed account of the experiences of the British and French soldiers who fought in the Suez action.
Carlton, David, *Anthony Eden, A Biography*, Allen Lane, 1981.
Charlwood, David, *Churchill and Eden*, Pen and Sword, 2020: the Suez Crisis was Anthony Eden's downfall. Not only has Suez come to define his legacy, but it has also coloured the perception of his entire career. In *Churchill and Eden* I explore the relationship between Anthony and Eden and Winston Churchill from their first meeting to the end their lives – the first book to do so. It provides valuable context for understanding Eden's actions during the Suez Crisis.
Chester, J. Pach, Jr, and Elmo Richardson, *The Presidency of Dwight D, Eisenhower*, University Press of Kansas, 1991.
Dutton, David, *Anthony Eden, A Life and Reputation*, Hodder, 1997.
Eden, Anthony, *Full Circle*, Cassell & Co., 1960: Eden's own memoir of the crisis is, it is fair to say, rather selective. Eden secured a deal with *The Times* to write multiple books recounting his career in politics and had wished for them to be published chronologically, but *The Times* insisted that the Suez volume be published first. Barely four years

on from the raw emotion of the crisis itself, while government documents remained classified, it was hardly surprising he produced a self-serving memoir. Thorpe, Eden's foremost biographer, insightfully notes, "One of the disadvantages for Eden of the sequence of his publications was that it contributed to a tendency from the 1960s onwards to assess his career backwards." It has done Eden no favours.

Fawcet, Louise, *International Relations of the Middle East*, Oxford University Press, 2009.

Fisk, Robert, *The Great War for Civilisation: The Conquest of the Middle East*, Fourth Estate, 2005.

Hoopes, Townsend, *The Devil and John Foster Dulles*, André Deutsch, 1974.

Immerman, Richard, H., *John Foster Dulles, Piety, Pragmatism and Power in U.S. Foreign Policy*, Scholarly Resources Inc, 1999.

Immerman, Richard, H. (ed), *John Foster Dulles and the Diplomacy of the Cold War*, Princeton University Press, 1990.

Kaufman, Burton, *The Arab Middle East and the United States*, Twayne, 1996.

Kinross, Lord, *Between Two Seas: The Creation of the Suez Canal*, John Murray, 1968: the inimitable Lord Kinross's account of the building of the Suez Canal, although half a century old, is still unsurpassed as a gripping storytelling of the cutting of the isthmus of Suez.

Kyle, Keith, *Suez: Britain's End of Empire in the Middle East*, I. B. Tauris, 2003: Kyle's extensive work is a key volume on the crisis. It covers in some depth the machinations at the UN, the relationship between Israel, Britain and France and the wider political fallout of the crisis in Britain and the U.S.

Lamb, Richard, *The Failure of the Eden Government*, Sidgwick and Jackson, 1987.

Love, Kennet, *Suez: The Twice Fought War*, McGraw-Hill, 1969: Love's epic work of history looks at both Suez conflicts: in 1956 and 1967.

McMahon, Robert, J., *Dean Acheson and the Creation of an American World Order*, Potomac Books, 2009.

Melanson, Richard and David Mayers, *Reevaluating Eisenhower: American Foreign Policy in the 1950s*, University of Illinois Press, 1987.

Mohammed, H. Heikal, *Cutting the Lion's Tail: Suez through Egyptian Eyes*, André Deutsch, 1986 is a valuable insight into the Egyptian perspective on Suez. Nasser was always far more open to Western influence than he was portrayed as being and it is almost always forgotten that a peaceful UN resolution to the Suez Crisis would in all likelihood have been achievable in the absence of French pressure for military action. The Suez Crisis goes by a different name in Egypt: it is known as 'the Tripartite Aggression', an arguably far more accurate description of events, as far as the Egyptians, the Americans and almost everyone other than the British, French and Israelis were concerned.

Neff, Donald, *Warriors at Suez, Eisenhower Takes America into the Middle East in 1956*, Amana Books, 1988 is a well-told narrative of the crisis by the recently deceased American journalist Donald Neff, which focuses on the events that led up to the triggering of the crisis in July 1956.

Nichols, David, A., *Eisenhower 1956: The President's Year of Crisis: Suez and the Brink of War,* Simon and Schuster, 2011: 1956 was a difficult year for Eisenhower. While it is now clear that the Politburo did not want all-out war over Suez or Hungary, the actors at the time did not have the historian's benefit of hindsight and access to sources from both sides. The best Eisenhower had were the grainy aerial photographs of Soviet airfields taken by U-2 spy planes. Nichols's book adroitly assesses the effect of the turn of events on Eisenhower's administration and fleshes out the highly charged context of facing down two world crises while running for re-election at home.

Rothwell, Victor, *Anthony Eden: A Political Biography, 1931-1957,* Manchester University Press, 1992.

Shlaim, Avi, *The Iron Wall, Israel and the Arab World,* Allen Lane, 2000.

Shuckburgh, Evelyn, *Descent to Suez, Diaries 1951–56,* Weidenfeld and Nicholson, 1986: Evelyn Shuckburgh was the Foreign Office official in charge of Middle Eastern affairs in 1956 and prior to 1954 had been Eden's private secretary. His diaries, although patchy during the crisis itself, give an intriguing perspective from a man who knew Eden well. It was Shuckburgh who recorded in his diary the entry ending "Petrol is up by one and sixpence."

Speller, I., *The Role of Amphibious Warfare in British Defence Policy, 1945–1956,* Palgrave Macmillan, 2001.

Takehy, Ray, *The Origins of the Eisenhower Doctrine: The U.S., Britain and Nasser's Egypt, 1953–57,* Palgrave Macmillan, 2000.

Thomas, Evan, *Ike's Bluff, President Eisenhower's Secret Battle to Save the World,* Little Brown, 2012 places Suez in the context of Eisenhower's presidency and eloquently narrates how the British and French action came across on the other side of 'The Pond'. Thomas also highlights the CIA's and Dulles's efforts to lure Nasser onto the Western side in the Cold War and the misstep over the Aswan Dam; when it came to Suez, he rightly attests, "The mess was part of America's making."

Tignor, Robert L., *Egypt: A Short History,* Princeton University Press, 2010.

Thorpe, D. R., *Eden: The Life and Times of Anthony Eden First Earl of Avon, 1897–1977,* Random House, 2011 is to date the most nuanced portrayal of Eden's complex professional and private life. Thorpe is Eden's foremost biographer.

Toye, Richard, *Churchill's Empire,* Macmillan, 2010.

Tunzelman, Alex von, *Blood and Sand: Suez, Hungary and the Crisis that Shook the World,* Simon and Schuster, 2016: the depth and breadth of the impact of the simultaneous crisis in Suez and Hungary is impossible to convey in a short book focused solely on Suez, but it is perhaps truest to state that the British were preoccupied with Suez while the Russians were preoccupied with Hungary. The Soviet invasion of Hungary proved Soviet paranoia over its position in Eastern Europe and that, as far as the Russians were concerned, events in the Middle East came a distant second to a threatened realignment on their doorstep. Alex von Tunzelman's excellent book does what it has been impossible to do in this volume and fully assesses the crises side by side.

Vassiliev, Alexei, *Russian policy in the Middle East: from Messianism to pragmatism*, Ithaca, 1994.
Wheelock, Keith, *Nasser's New Egypt, a Critical Analysis*, Greenwood Press, 1960.
Yapp, M. E., *The Making of the Modern Near East 1792–1923*, Longman, 1987.
Zelikow, Philip and Ernest R. May, *Suez Deconstructed: An Interactive Study in Crisis, War and Peacemaking*, Brookings Institution Press, 2019 breaks down the narrative of the crisis into the responses of the different administrations in London, Washington, Cairo, Moscow and Jerusalem. In particular it provides a valuable insight into French and Egyptian perspectives.

## PHOTOGRAPHIC COPYRIGHT INFORMATION

Eisenhower portrait; Library of Congress, Prints and Photographs Division, photograph by Fabian Bachrach, [LC-USZ62-117123].
Israeli representatives, Cohen, Fritz, Israeli National Photo Collection, Government Press Office.
Molotov, Churchill and Eden, Department of Foreign Affairs and Trade, Australia, www.dfat.gov.au, CC BY 3.0 AU.
Israeli troops leaving Suez, Milner, Moshe, Israeli National Photo Collection, Government Press Office.
Prisoners of war, Moshe Pridan, Israeli National Photo Collection, Government Press Office.
Ben-Gurion portrait, Cohen, Fritz, Israeli National Photo Collection, Government Press Office.
Moshe Dayan portrait, Herman Chanania, Israeli National Photo Collection, Government Press Office.
Golda Meir speech, Milner, Moshe, Israeli National Photo Collection, Government Press Office.
Abba Eban portrait, Fritz Cohen, Israeli National Photo Collection, Government Press Office.
Israeli Mystères, David Eldon, Israeli National Photo Collection, Government Press Office.
Israeli AMX tanks, Israeli National Photo Collection, Government Press Office.
Israeli paratroops training, David Eldon, Israeli National Photo Collection, Government Press Office.
Paratroops Mitla Pass, Vered Avraham, Israeli National Photo Collection, Government Press Office.
Israeli reprisals, Moshe Milner, Israeli National Photo Collection, Government Press Office.
Israeli paratroops DC-3, Israeli National Photo Collection, Government Press Office.
Israeli children and nannies, Israeli Defense Forces, Nir Eliyahu Archive.
Sharon and Chirac, Amos Ben, Gershom, Israeli National Photo Collection, Government Press Office.
Israeli armoured column, Israeli National Photo Collection, Government Press Office.
Egyptian guns, Moshe Milner, Israeli National Photo Collection, Government Press Office.
Pineau and Ben-Gurion. Pridan, Mosche, Israeli National Photo Collection, Government Press Office.
Sharm el-Sheikh flag, Israeli National Photo Collection, Government Press Office.
Nixon and Khrushchev, Special Media Archives Services Division, RG306-RMN-1-21.
Canberra; Open Government Licence, SAC A K Benson/MOD.

Stalin statue head, Fortepan adományozó, Hofbauer, Robert, licenced under CC BY-SA 3.0.

MiG-15, צור קיסריה-יהודה בן. יהודה בן-צור קיסריה, CC BY-SA 3.0.

Guy Mollet, National Archief, Dutch National Archives, CC BY-SA 3.0 NL.

Palestinian Fedayeen, Tiamet, licenced under CC BY-SA 3.0.

Suez Canal buildings 1910, Library of Congress, Prints and Photographs Division, [LC-DIG-ggbain-17718].

Opening of Suez Canal illumination, Library of Congress, Prints and Photographs Division, [LC-USZ62-95901].

Suez Canal Ismalia, Library of Congress, Prints and Photographs Division, [LC-DIG-matpc-15896].

Canal Company Offices, Library of Congress, Prints and Photographs Division, [LC-DIG-ggbain-00553].

Mitla Pass, Library of Congress, Prints and Photographs Division, [LC-DIG-matpc-15553].

Baghdad Pact poster, Series: Propaganda Posters Distributed in Asia, Latin America and the Middle East, ca. 1950–ca. 1965 Record Group 306: Records of the U.S. Information Agency, 1900–2003, U.S. National Archives, 6948821.

Eisenhower and Dulles, White House Albums, 1953–1961 Record Group 79: Records of the National Park Service, 1785–2006, U.S. National Archives, 594350.

Ambulance car being lowered from flight deck, RAMC 1187, Wellcome Images.

Suez Canal near the town of Kantara, Gan-Shmuel archive via PikiWiki Israel.

Avenue de Lesseps. "May 1942 – Avenue De Lesseps in magnificent French Gardens, Ismailia, Egypt – real photo card (circa 1930s)" by assuejeff, licensed under CC BY 2.0.

"May 1942 – Heavily laden southbound dhows on the Suez Canal, with passengers & livestock waiting for the Kantara ferry at the El Kantara West bank wharf, Egypt" by assuejeff, licensed under CC BY 2.0.

"25 Feb 1942 – "N. 4113 – Port Said – Prince Farouk Street", Egypt – real photo post card – circa 1930s" by assuejeff, licensed under CC BY 2.0.

"March 1942 – Local Arab men & boys in one of the bustling side alleys of downtown Cairo, Egypt" by assuejeff, licensed under CC BY 2.0.

"Vietnam war 1965" by manhai, CC BY 2.0.

An Israeli officer at Mitla Pass. Israeli Defense Forces Spokesperson's Unit, Government Press Office.

*Al-Ahram* front page 29 July 1956; *Al-Ahram* front page 30 October 1956; *Al-Ahram* newspaper; Bush and Blair; FLN Algeria; British carriers, cover image; Carrier, Personnel Half-Track M3 (Alan Wilson); Chequers; Czech arms deal; Clarissa and Eden, Dag Hammarskjöld; de Lesseps statue; Dayan address; de Lesseps; HMS *Eagle*, *Bulwark* and *Albion*; Destroyed Egyptian planes Six-Day War; Six-Day War; John Foster Dulles; Eisenhower portrait; Imre Nagy; John Bagot Glubb; Inchas airfield following an attack by Fleet Air Arm Sea Hawks; F-84; Logistical mess; King Hussein 1953; Kuwait oil fires; Nasser speech nationalizing canal; Port Said tanks; Nasser 1960 Mansouria; HMS *Theseus* helicopters; Il-28 bombers; Geneva Conference; Troops of 3rd Battalion Parachute Regiment escort a captured

## Sources

Egyptian soldier; Sea Venom; Knocked-out Sherman tank in the Sinai; Port Said from the air, 5 November 1956; A British Centurion tank; Paras from the 3rd Battalion land at El Gamil Airfield, Port Said; Westland Whirlwinds taking off from HMS *Theseus*, UN in Egypt; U.S. tanks; Soviet postcard; Napoleon in Egypt; Suez Bay, Egypt, 1856; House of Ferdinand de Lesseps (Pierre cb); Egyptian military forces guard post at the brink of the Suez Canal (Heb); Port Said, Suez Canal Authority (Daniel Csörföly); The Royal Navy battleship HMS *Howe*; The amphibious assault ship, USS *Kearsarge* (C.J. Newsome); Soviet armour in Budapest (Fortepan); A caricature of Le Vicomte de Lesseps, the original caption reading: "He suppressed an isthmus." Vanity Fair, 27 November 1869.; Thirteen years after the opening of the canal, Britain went to war in Egypt to safeguard shipping and put down the nationalist Urabi revolt; Port Said, the Arab Quarter, 1890; Port Said, the port, 1890; De Havilland Sea Venom FAW22 (DH-112) seen in the markings of 809 Naval Air Squadron during the Suez Crisis of 1956; Ian Fleming's villa in Jamaica which he lent to Eden in November 1956; Harold Macmillan pictured with John F. Kennedy five years after the Suez Crisis; The US circumvented the power of the British and French vetoes in the UN Security Council by securing a resolution against the Suez action in the General Assembly; Nasser with his children, May 1956. Five months later on Abdul's fifth birthday (pictured far right), Israel invaded the Sinai; Nasser and Khrushchev pictured at the diverting of the Nile for construction of the Aswan dam; Said Pasha, whom de Lesseps convinced to help fund and provide workers for the construction of the canal; Selwyn Lloyd (far left) as Foreign Secretary in 1960, seen here with other European foreign ministers; Moshe Dayan addresses the IDF's 9th Brigade at Sharm el-Sheikh after the Sinai campaign; Israeli generals Haim Laskov, Moshe Kashti, Asaf Simchoni and Dan Tolkovski in Sinai, 1956; A 1914 map of Port Said and environs, including the port facilities (1:50,000), with an inserted smaller map of the actual city (1:25,000) – labelled in French; The entrance to the canal at Port Said, 1856; During the Suez crisis in 1956, the cartoonist Ronald Searle (the creator of St. Trinian's School) was commissioned to do the artwork for a set of leaflets that was to be dropped over Egyptian support of the invasion by British and French troops; Nasser receiving the Indian military delegation at the presidency, February 1956; President Nasser raises the Egyptian flag over the local naval headquarters at Port Said in celebration of the British military withdrawal from the canal zone a few days prior, 18 June 1956; British troops distribute food in Port Said, 12 November 1956; Jordanian Army Chief of Staff Radi Annab standing next to Nasser during Friday prayers in the last week of Ramadan, 4 May 1956; The Royal Navy minesweeper HMS *Bossington* (M1133) during operations in the Suez Canal, 1974; King Hussein of Jordan (left), President Nasser of Egypt and his Chief of Staff Abdel Hakim Amer before signing the Egyptian–Jordanian–Iraqi defence pact in Cairo, May 1967; Officers of the Lancashire Fusiliers at Kasr el Nil Barracks, Cairo, 1898. They are wearing red roses on their pith helmets to commemorate the defeat of the French at Minden on 1 August 1759; Sudanese prisoners in chains carry the baggage of British soldiers (probably 21st Lancers) through the streets of Wadi Halfa, during Kitchener's campaign of 1898; Egyptian troop deployment: *Wikimedia Commons*.

# Index

2nd Colonial Parachute Regiment (French) 93

Abdullah, King (of Jordan) 67
Al-Arish 85
Alexandria 12, 17, 22, 40, 53, 58
Algerian insurgency *also* FLN 45, 46, 49, 58, 93, 108
Anglo-Egyptian Treaty (1954) 5, 16
Anglo-Jordanian Treaty 7, 68, 69, 114
Arab-Israeli wars 25, 26, 68, 111, 113
    Israeli war of independence (1948) 25, 26, 68
    Six-Day War (1967) 111, 113
arms deals 6, 17, 20, 21, 27, 29
    to Egypt 6, 17, 20, 21, 27
    to Israel 29
Aswan Dam 6, 17, 21, 29, 38, 55, 56, 111

Baghdad Pact 21, 67
BBC *see* British Broadcasting Corporation
Ben-Gurion, David 7, 25, 27-29, 43, 45, 57-61, 67, 72, 76, 78, 82, 93, 102, 103, 111
bin Laden, Osama 115
Birch, Nigel 40
Blair, Tony 115-119
Bonaparte, Napoleon 8, 9
British Broadcasting Corporation 22, 34, 105
Brown, Gordon 119
Budapest *see* Hungarian uprising
Bulganin, Nikolai 29, 30, 82, 97, 100, 104
Bush, George W. 115, 116fn
Butler, Rab 61

Cabinet (British) 12, 15, 18, 29, 34, 40, 49, 61, 65, 68, 94, 97, 98, 100, 101, 106, 107, 110, 115
Cairo International Airport, bombing of 78
Cairo Radio 68, 85
Central Intelligence Agency 40, 44, 79, 92, 104
Cheney, Dick 116
Churchill, Winston 11, 14, 15, 34, 41, 42, 44, 62, 64, 106
Cold War 17, 20, 21, 22, 30, 43, 111, 116
Communist Party (Soviet) 29
Compagnie universelle du canal maritime de Suez 8

Conservative Party (British) 56, 96
Cook, Robin 115

Dayan, Moshe 25-29, 43, 44, 54, 55, 58-60, 67, 72, 81, 85, 101-103, 111
de Gaulle, Charles 112
de Lesseps, Ferdinand 8-12, 19, 23, 98, 109, 110, 114
Dean, Patrick 59-61
Dulles, John Foster 6, 19, 20-22, 29, 33-35, 43, 44, 49-51, 53, 55, 56, 61, 64-66, 74, 79, 89, 90, 97, 106, 111, 114

Eban, Abba 59, 75, 76
Eden, Anthony 6, 7, 12, 14-19, 22, 33, 34, 36, 39-46, 49-51, 56-59, 61-65, 69, 74-76, 82, 84, 87, 90, 91, 94, 96, 97, 98, 100, 101, 104-107, 109-112, 114, 118, 119
Egyptian Air Force 41, 42, 55, 76, 78, 83, 84, 113
Egyptian Army 14, 87, 93
Eisenhower Doctrine 7, 111
Eisenhower, Dwight D. 6, 7, 16, 18-22, 29, 33-35, 43, 44, 49, 55, 56, 61, 65, 66, 74, 75, 78, 79, 82, 89, 90, 92, 94, 104, 105, 111
El Gamil airfield 93, 94

Fawsi, Mahmoud 52, 53, 55, 56
*fedayeen* 26, 27, 59, 68
Foreign Office (British) 10, 14, 21, 36, 41, 57, 59, 68, 75, 91, 110
French Indochina *see* Vietnam

Gaza 29
*Georges Leygues* (French cruiser) 85
Gilles, Gen Jean 93
Glubb, John Bagot 67, 68
Golda Meir 54, 55, 59, 72

Heath, Edward 61
Hungarian uprising 62-66, 79, 82, 83, 91, 104, 112
Hussein, King (of Jordan) 68, 69, 71, 114
Hussein, Saddam 115, 116, 119

International Monetary Fund 106, 107
Ismailia 23, 75

*Index*

Israeli Defense Forces 6, 7, 26-28, 65, 68, 69, 72, 73, 75, 76, 81, 84-87, 95, 99, 102, 109, 112, 113, 115
   202 Brigade 85, 115
   Israeli Air Force 28, 69, 72, 73, 76, 78, 102, 111

Joint Chiefs of Staff (U.S.) 104
Joint Intelligence Committee (British) 59, 100

Khrushchev, Nikita 29, 30, 35, 38, 63, 64, 66, 82, 105, 111, 112

Labour Party (British) 111, 115
Lloyd, Selwyn 7, 41, 44, 46, 47, 49, 51-53, 55, 56, 58, 59, 62, 66, 69, 74, 100, 106, 107
Lodge, Henry Cabot 91
London conferences 6, 34, 42-44, 49, 51, 52
Luxor air base 83

Macmillan, Harold 40, 61, 97, 100, 101, 106, 107
Mayo, 2Lt Peter 69, 93, 99, 109
Menzies, Robert 6, 35, 42
Mitla Pass 73, 74, 81, 84, 85, 115
Mollet, Guy 45, 51, 61, 82, 84, 101, 106, 112
Molotov, Vyacheslav 63, 64, 82

Nagy, Imre 63, 64, 66, 83, 91, 112
Nasser, Gamal Abdel 6, 12-14, 16-22, 25, 27-30, 33-38, 40, 42-46, 49, 51-58, 60, 61, 68, 70, 71, 73, 75, 78, 79, 80, 82, 85, 88, 90, 91, 93, 94, 108-112, 116
National Security Council (NSC) (U.S.) 21, 29, 65, 89, 106

Operation *Cordage* 69
Operation *Musketeer* 41, 42, 52, 53, 69, 98
Organization for European Economic Cooperation 106
Ottoman Empire 8, 11

Palestinian militants *see fedayeen*
Panama Canal 20, 51, 110
Parachute Brigade Group (British) 41
   3rd Parachute Battalion 93, 95
Peres, Shimon 61
Pineau, Christian 22, 33, 43-47, 49-51, 53-60, 62, 87, 101, 106, 112
Politburo (Soviet) 29, 46, 62-64, 66, 83, 105, 112
Port Fuad 93

Port Said 6, 7, 9, 16, 18, 31, 32, 37, 40, 42, 49, 53, 75, 76, 87, 92, 93, 96-98, 100, 101, 105, 108-110

Quai d'Orsay 61

Republican Party (U.S.) 43
Royal Air Force 40, 41, 58, 74, 78, 83
Royal Navy (Mediterranean Fleet) 40, 42, 76, 78, 86
   Fleet Air Arm 78, 86
   HMS *Albion* 39, 76
   HMS *Ark Royal* 42
   HMS *Bulwark* 39, 76
   HMS *Eagle* 39, 76
   HMS *Ocean* 92, 98
   HMS *Simla* 69
   HMS *Theseus* 92, 98
   Royal Marines 42, 69, 76, 92, 93, 98, 99
      42 Commando 69, 76, 92, 93

Said Pasha 8, 10, 23
Sèvres 58-61, 72, 74, 76, 84, 102, 106, 110
   Protocol 6, 61, 74, 76, 84, 106, 110
Sharm el-Sheikh 81, 101-104
Sharon, Ariel 85, 115, 116
Sinai Desert 29, 38, 55, 57, 59, 72-74, 76, 84, 85, 93, 94, 99, 101, 111
Stalin, Joseph 29, 62, 63
State Department (U.S.) 17, 21, 51, 74, 91
Stockwell, Gen Sir Hugh 105
Suez Canal Company 7, 10, 12, 18, 34, 49, 56, 99, 109
Suez Canal Users' Association (SCUA) 6, 44, 49, 51

Treaty of Rome 112

United Nations 6, 21, 43, 44, 49-53, 55, 56, 58, 59, 66, 68, 74, 75, 87, 90, 91, 94, 97, 107-109, 112, 117, 118
   General Assembly 90
      resolution 1441 117, 118
      resolution 997 ES-1 89-95
   peacekeeping force 94, 109, 112
   Security Council 6, 49, 51, 66, 68, 75, 90

Vietnam 17, 50, 71, 93, 111

Wilson, Harold 71, 111

**David Charlwood** obtained a First Class Honours Degree in history from Royal Holloway, University of London, and has worked as an international journalist and in publishing. His research into the early twentieth-century Middle East has been published in the *British Journal of Middle Eastern Studies* and he has also been a contributing historian for BBC radio. He is the author of four books and writes for Pen and Sword's Cold War 1945–1991 and History of Terror series.

*Also from David Charlwood*
**A moving, gripping short history of the 'forgotten genocide', told through the stories of those who witnessed it.**

Crammed into cattle trucks and deported to camps, shot and buried in mass graves, or force-marched to death: over 1.5 million Armenians were murdered by the Turkish state, twenty years before the start of Hitler's Holocaust. It was described as a crime against humanity and Turkey was condemned by Russia, France, Great Britain and the United States. But two decades later the genocide had been conveniently forgotten. Hitler justified his Polish death squads by asking in 1939: "Who after all is today speaking about the destruction of the Armenians?" *Armenian Genocide* is a new, gripping short history that tells the story of a forgotten genocide: the men and women who died, the few who survived, and the diplomats who tried to intervene.

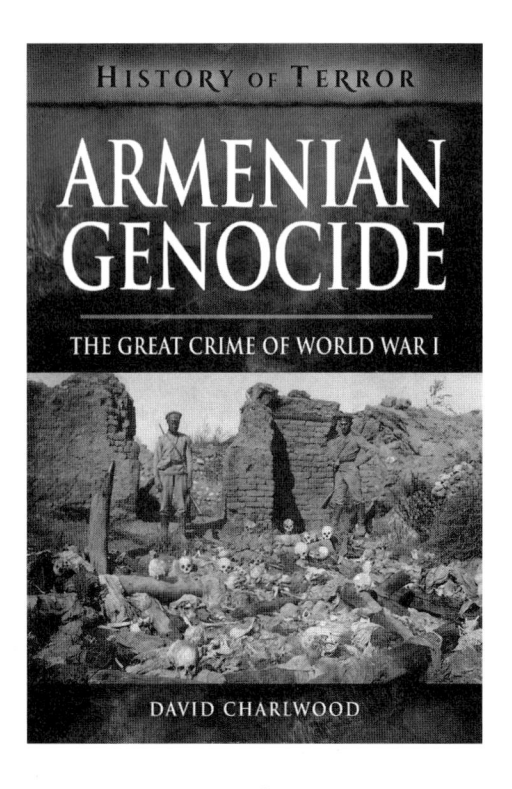